PRAI/E FOR FEMALE, GIFTED & BLACK

"A powerful resource for young Black girls to empower themselves with the stories of their foremothers. The Black women in this book will guide and lead future generations to recognize that they have the love, strength, and ferocity to change their world."

—**Karen Arrington**, author of *Your Next Level Life: 7 Rules of Power, Confidence, and Opportunity for Black Women in America*

"No matter how much you think you know about the awesomeness of Black women, this book will give you more reasons to celebrate what Black women have done and are destined to do. This book is a balm and a healing for all who will read it."

—**Marita Golden**, author of *The Strong Black Woman: How a Myth Endangers the Physical and Mental Health of Black Women*

"The world needs more works celebrating the excellence of strong, accomplished Black women! This is an excellent introduction to those who've earned their places in history."

—**Chrisanne Beckner**, architectural historian, writer, and author of *100 African Americans Who Shaped American History*

"Black women trailblazers who have paved the way for future generations of Black girls to build their own achievements, successes, and triumphs. Here are the foremothers whose stories and lives will help teach young Black girls the power they hold within to change and redefine social boundaries."

—**Varla Ventura**, author of *Sheroes: Bold, Brash, and Absolutely Unabashed Superwomen*

"A celebration of indomitable Black women who scaled centuries of oppression to reach the mountaintop. The encapsulated biographies prove that the impossible can be possible."

—**Marlene Wagman-Geller**, author of *Women of Means: The Fascinating Biographies of Royals, Heiresses, Eccentrics and Other Poor Little Rich Girls*

"We are honored by their lives, their stories, their grace and the inspirational precedent set for all to follow in their footsteps."

—**Bridgitte Jackson-Buckley**, interviewer, memoirist, and author of *The Gift of Crisis: How I Used Meditation to Go From Financial Failure to a Life of Purpose*

FEMALE, GIFTED & BLACK

OTHER BOOKS BY BECCA ANDERSON

Badass Affirmations

The Book of Awesome Women

The Book of Awesome Girls

The Book of Awesome Women Writers

Badass Women Give the Best Advice

You Are an Awesome Woman

Think Happy to Stay Happy

The Woman's Book of Prayer

Let Me Count the Ways

The Joy of Self-Care

The Crafty Gardener

Every Day Thankful

I Can Do Anything

OTHER BOOKS BY M.J. FIEVRE

Badass Black Girl: Quotes, Questions, and Affirmations for Teens

Empowered Black Girl: Joyful Affirmations and Words of Resilience

Resilient Black Girl: 52 Weeks of Anti-Racist Activities for Black Joy & Resilience

Black and Resilient: 52 Weeks of Anti-Racist Activities for Black Joy & Resilience

Walk Boldly: Empowerment Toolkit for Young Black Men

Happy, Okay? Poems about Anxiety, Depression, Hope and Survival

Raising Confident Black Kids: A Comprehensive Guide for Empowering Parents and Teachers of Black Children

Young Trailblazers: The Book of Black Inventors and Scientists

Young Trailblazers: The Book of Black Heroes and Groundbreakers

FEMALE, GIFTED & BLACK

Awesome Art and Literary Pioneers Who Changed the World

M.J. FIEVRE AND BECCA ANDERSON

mango
CORAL GABLES

Cover Design: Megan Werner
Layout & Design: Megan Werner

For permission requests, please contact the publisher at:
Mango Publishing Group
2850 S Douglas Road, 4th Floor
Coral Gables, FL 33134 USA
info@mango.bz

For special orders, quantity sales, course adoptions and corporate
sales, please email the publisher at sales@mango.bz. For trade and
wholesale sales, please contact Ingram Publisher Services at
customer.service@ingramcontent.com or +1.800.509.4887.

Female, Gifted & Black: Awesome Art and Literary Pioneers Who
Changed the World

Library of Congress Cataloging-in-Publication number: 2022944398
ISBN: (p) 978-1-68481-114-4 (e) 978-1-68481-115-1
BISAC category code: YAN006020, YOUNG ADULT NONFICTION /
Biography & Autobiography / Cultural, Ethnic & Regional

Contents

BEYOND ANY SIMPLISTIC NARRATIVE

Black women are natural leaders. They are the catalysts in the engine of change that transforms our homes, our communities, and our nations. In the struggle for civil rights in America, Black women have steadily led the way. It was Black women who led the Underground Railroad, pioneered the suffrage movement, organized the freedom riders, and paved the way for constitutional protections against sex discrimination.

A century ago, the 19th Amendment granted women the right to vote in America. It has taken far longer for women, and specifically Black women, to be granted a seat at the cultural and political tables of America. Black women are still underrepresented among political candidates in races across the nation, making up only 2 percent of challengers to incumbents. Yet they remain consistent in turning out to vote to defend the rights of marginalized people. Even as they are still far too often overlooked, unrecognized, or actively suppressed, however, Black women dare to overcome oppression, to break rules, to reimagine the world, to wage a rebellion. They are active in pushing for long-neglected reforms, creating a more equitable America, and securing their place at the table.

The perseverance of Black women is all around us—in politics, in sports, in the arts. It's blazing and it's consistent. Black women show up and fight for the common good. They spark crucial dialogue and reshape the future. Since Black women are not a monolith, it is necessary to showcase their contributions and lives far beyond any simplistic narrative. Our communities are infused with the spirit of Black women whose accomplishments serve as testaments to beauty, rhythm, joy, tragedy, heartbreak, and love.

In this book, we are proud to celebrate Black women in the creative world—musicians, actors, visual artists, writers, poets and literary pioneers, dancers, models, and other creators who used their talents to challenge social, racial, and sexual stereotypes across the globe. From legendary icons like singer Ella Fitzgerald and writer Octavia E. Butler to trailblazers like artist Augusta Savage and dancer Misty Copeland, we're proud to present various dynamic Black women who inspire us to achieve greatness.

M.J. Fievre, author of the Badass Black Girl series

Becca Anderson, author of *The Book of Awesome Women* and *The Book of Awesome Girls*

chapter one

AMAZING ARTISTS

Black women are on center stage today, standing on foundations built by trailblazers of previous generations who fought for the opportunity to perform, to be recorded, to get airplay, and just for a chance. For example, **Billie Holiday**, an enormous talent, struggled throughout her career and paid the price in ill-treatment she received as a Black woman for insisting on being taken seriously for her music.

Thankfully, things have changed. Women now retain the copyrights to their music, run their own record companies, call the shots, direct the videos, and manage their money with the strategic elan of MBAs. **Bessie Smith** went from busking for pennies on a Chattanooga streetcorner to riding in her own custom railcar to venues to perform. **Tina Turner** turned the tables on an abusive Svengali, Ike Turner, started meditating, and came back with a vengeance for an amazing career as a seemingly ageless R&B goddess; she has had a thriving career full of success and love. **Lena Horne** sued the nightclubs that discriminated against her at a time when Black women were used to sitting still and being quiet.

Offstage, the business of music has seen a power shift as well. **Sylvia Rhone** was the first Black woman ever to run a record company, Elektra, by pushing up through the ranks of an industry she describes as having a "pimp mentality." Today, several Black women are in the top ranks at Sony, MTV, and Epic Records. However, these women's success stories are cautionary tales of working within the constraints of boy's club corporations, where women are often mere window dressing or products are sold with an emphasis on sex. Rapper shero **Mary J. Blige** put it most succinctly with her cut-to-the-chase wisdom for women: "Don't let anybody stomp you out!"

Here are a few of the bravest, those who faced tremendous risks—often physical—in the pursuit of art.

PEGGY JONES:
Lady Bo

Peggy Jones was a woman who followed her own star, and in so doing, shattered a number of music industry stereotypes. She had music in her soul from the beginning; a dancer in her toddler years, she had performed at Carnegie Hall by the age of nine. As a youngster, the New Yorker was intrigued by the ukulele before moving on to the guitar. It never occurred to her that it would be unusual for a woman to play guitar in the forties. "Little did I know that a female playing any instrument was like a new thing. I was breaking a lot of barriers."

By the age of seventeen, she was producing and cutting singles such as "Honey Bunny Baby/Why Do I Love You?" and "Everybody's Talking/I'm Gonna Love My Way." In the late fifties, she and her friends and future husband Bobby Bakersfield formed The Jewels, a band made up of men and women, which was very unusual for the time; even more unique, the band included both Black and white members. The Jewels got a lot of flack for their disregard for gender and racial barriers, but they persisted in performing to enthusiastic audiences. Jones recalls fighting past the objections: "I just hung in there because this is what I wanted to do, and I had a real strong constitution as to the way I thought I should go about it."

Jones's singular instrumentation was one of the sonic ingredients of Bo Diddley's successful albums and national tours throughout the fifties and sixties. Diddley, famous for his signature rhythm, saw Jones walking down the street with her guitar one day; ever the savvy showman, he recognized that having a pretty girl playing guitar in his band would be a very good thing for ticket and record sales. Jones was ushered into the world of professional musicianship full-time with Diddley's touring band. She learned a great deal, perfecting her guitar playing to the point where Diddley himself was a bit threatened by her hot licks. She also saw the hardships of the road and experienced firsthand the color line that mandated discriminatory treatment even for music stars. When they hit the South in the hearses that were their tour transports, the band often had to say in hotels designated for nonwhite people and had to use separate bathrooms for "coloreds." They even had to figure out a way to cook in the car when they couldn't find a restaurant that would serve Black people.

However, Jones wasn't content with just backup and liner note credits and took a hiatus from the nonstop Bo Diddley roadshow. She again wrote her own material and performed with The Jewels. Then, in the late sixties, she formed her own band and went out on the road. Peggy Jones was a true pioneer for women in music. Because of her, the idea of a woman playing guitar—or any instrument in a band—became much more acceptable.

> "I don't think I went in with any attitude that 'Oh, oh, I'm a girl, they're not going to like my playing.' So probably that might have been my savior, because I just went in as a musician and expected to be accepted as a musician."
>
> **—Peggy Jones**

BEYONCÉ KNOWLE/-CARTER:

Flawless

Born in 1981 in Houston, Texas, in 1990, **Beyoncé** joined the all-female R&B group Girl's Tyme, which after a few false starts under various names, became Destiny's Child by 1996. After success with several chart-topping Destiny's Child singles, her first solo album was released in 2003 and she has never looked back. She married hip-hop artist Jay-Z in 2008; they had a daughter named Blue Ivy in 2012, followed by twins Rumi and Sir in 2017. She has performed twice at the Super Bowl and sang the national anthem at President Obama's second inauguration.

In a 2013 interview with *Vogue*, Beyoncé said that she thought of herself as "a modern-day feminist." She also sampled "We should all be feminists" from a TEDx talk in 2013 by Nigerian author Chimamanda Ngozi Adichie in her song of that year, "Flawless," although she has critics who feel her racy performances are not supportive of women's empowerment.

Since the rise of the Black Lives Matter movement, Beyoncé and her husband have donated millions to it, as well as contributing to the Ban Bossy campaign, which seeks to encourage leadership in girls via social and other media. She also included the mothers of Trayvon Martin, Michael Brown, and Eric Garner in the video for her song "Freedom" holding pictures of their unjustly murdered sons. In April of 2016, Beyoncé released a visual album called *Lemonade* as an HBO special. In it, she showed the strength found in communities of African American women as well as in women in general. *Lemonade* debuted at number one, as did her 2022 album *Renaissance*, making Beyoncé the only artist in history to have all of her seven studio albums reach the top of *Billboard*'s album charts.

ARETHA FRANKLIN:
Earning Our Respect

A preacher's daughter, **Aretha Franklin** started her musical career early, appearing with her famous dad, Revered Clarence LaVaugh Franklin, at Detroit's New Baptist Church. She was born an obviously talented musician who willingly passed up piano lessons so she could experiment with her own style of playing. By the age of eight, Franklin electrified her father's congregation in 1950 with her first gospel solo; by fourteen, she'd cut her first gospel record, *Songs of*

Faith. Encouraged by her father and his circle of friends and acquaintances, which included Dinah Washington, Reverend James Cleveland, Mahalia Jackson, Clara Ward, Sam Cooke, and Art Tatum, the budding gospel great had her eyes on the glittery prize of pop stardom. She decided to move to New York to pursue her dream in 1960.

Her album *Aretha* was released by Columbia the next year, positioning her as a jazz artist with her covers of classics like "God Bless the Child," "Ol' Man River," and "Over the Rainbow." Franklin went on to record ten albums with Columbia, while record execs waffled about how to package her. Jerry Wexler of Atlantic Records was a fan of Franklin and signed her immediately when her contract with Columbia ran out. Wexler rightly saw Franklin as an R&B singer; she agreed. Her debut album with Atlantic, *I Never Loved a Man*, contained "Respect," a crossover hit which catapulted Franklin to number one on both the pop and R&B charts. "Respect" became an anthem in 1967 for both feminists and Black activists.

"Respect" was just the beginning of a chain of hits for the singer: "Baby, I Love You," "Natural Woman," and "Chain of Fools" came hot on the heels of the international smash hit, and soon Franklin was dubbed the "Queen of Soul," reigning over the music world for decades with the power and authority of her god-given gift.

Aretha Franklin was inspired to sing, rather than be the church pianist, when she heard Clara Ward. "From then on, I knew what I wanted to do—sing! I liked all of Miss Ward's records." She also idolized Dinah Washington and recorded a tribute album in 1964 after Washington's tragic death in her prime. Much like what Washington herself had done for Bessie Smith, Franklin created an amazing and moving set of covers to honor the brilliance and glory of the Detroit diva entitled "Unforgettable." And it is—as was Aretha's 1985 duet with Annie Lennox, summing up the sherodom of these legends among women: "Sisters Are Doin' It for Themselves." Amen, sisters!

DINAH WASHINGTON:
Legendary Voice

Rolling Stone journalist Gerry Hershey makes the claim, "If there is a paramount body for evidence to support the feminist poster 'Sisterhood is powerful,' it is **Dinah Washington**'s 1958 LP tribute to the Empress, *The Bessie Smith Songbook*." Washington was one of the all-time great vocalists, a singer who immediately took ownership of any song she sang. In addition to a great set of pipes, she had a good head for business, running a restaurant in Detroit as well as a booking agency called Queen Attractions, where she signed talent like Muhammad Ali and Sammy Davis Jr. Apparently able to simultaneously juggle many different avenues of expression, Washington also dominated the stage of the Flame Show Bar and Detroit's Twenty Grand Club, where future superstars Marvin Gaye, Diana Ross, and Aretha Franklin sat enthralled, watching a master at work. Motown was just gearing up when Washington died accidentally of an unfortunate combination of pills and alcohol. A legend in her own time, she is rumored to have married as many as nine times before her untimely demise at age thirty-nine. Dinah Washington, one of the most gifted singers ever to have held a microphone, lived large, predating the rock-star excesses of later generations!

QUEEN LATIFAH:
Playing with the Big Boys

When Jersey girl Dana Owens renamed herself **Queen Latifah** and started rapping, she broke barriers in the very male world of hip-hop. Taking up the mantle of an African Queen, her music efforts—*Ladies First*, *All Hail the Queen*, *Nature of A Sista'*, and *Black Reign*—proved to everyone that women could rap and could do it well, as well as draw a huge audience across gender lines. Queen Latifah then crossed over into acting, starring in the popular television series *Living Single* and in feature films like *Set It Off*, *Jungle Fever*, *Juice*, and the hit musical *Chicago* just for starters.

She paved the way for a new wave of female rappers, including breakout hip-hop stars Foxy Brown and Lil' Kim, with the intention of establishing a woman-positive place within the musical style she claimed was to the eighties and nineties what rock and roll was to the fifties and sixties. In early 2021, Latifah rose to the occasion with her starring role in *The Equalizer*, which as of the summer of 2022 had been renewed by CBS for a third season—all hail the queen coming up in a fierce action/adventure series!

> **"My thing was to start with the ladies and get the self-esteem up."**
>
> **—Queen Latifah,**
> American rapper, singer, songwriter, actress, and producer; she was a key player in reshaping the rap industry to make space for women rappers

---

Black singing in America began in the fields with slaves who sang call-and-response songs and work songs to one another to pass the time. Often, white plantation owners, fearing the native languages of their slaves could be used to communicate secretly and provoke uprisings, forbade their slaves to sing in their own languages. As the slave population converted to Christianity, the field songs changed from songs of work to spirituals and hymns, all sung in call-and-response, where a soloist sings out a line of the song and then those around the singer repeat the line back in the song's rhythm, followed by a refrain.

Black song began to influence mainstream America in the nineteenth century with the rise of blackface minstrel shows incorporating some of the melodies of Black song in their stage performances. After the Civil War, groups of Black singers organized and went on tour. The Fisk University Singers may have been the first, going on tour in 1871 and earning enough money for a building on the Fisk University campus that was named Jubilee Hall. The Hyers Sisters Comic Opera Company was organized in 1876. It was the first Black musical comedy troupe ever to perform. The barbershop was a popular place for people to socialize, and Black American singers performing in four-part harmony popularized the barbershop quartet.

Black musical theater had its debut on Broadway in 1898 with a musical by Bob Cole and Billy Johnson. In 1901, the first recording of Black singers was made of Bert Williams and George Walker, whose selections featured music from Broadway musicals. The first Black opera company, the Drury Opera Company, was founded in 1900. The opera company's orchestra was composed of all white classical musicians, but the singers featured onstage were Black opera singers. The company lasted less than a decade, until 1908. Scott Joplin was very popular during this era as well and produced *Treemonisha*, a ragtime-folk opera first performed in 1911.

In the 1920s and 1930s, jazz and blues became popular, leading to the careers of musicians such as Louis Armstrong, Jelly

Roll Morton, and Duke Ellington. In the 1940s, white singers began recording covers of Black songs and hitting the charts with their versions of Black music. Black vocalists were left to perform for all-Black audiences, often with little or no mainstream success.

In 1955, Thurman Ruth convinced a gospel group to perform outside of a church setting at the Apollo Theater. The act was so popular they ended up going on tour, performing at clubs and other venues traditionally reserved for rhythm and blues singers.

Black singers popularized rock and roll music, but it was mainly white performers who benefitted; Chuck Berry and Bo Diddly, however, managed to buck that trend and found popular success. **Sister Rosetta Thorpe** tore up the stage with her electric guitar and electrified singing voice in the 1950s. She influenced a generation of vocalists, including Aretha Franklin. Fats Domino was also popular during this era, though he claimed rock and roll was just rhythm and blues. Doo-wop became popular in the 1950s with its harmonized vocalizations and nonsense words. Singing sirens **Etta James**, **Gladys Knight**, **Nina Simone**, **Patti LaBelle**, **Roberta Flack**, **Diana Ross**, and **Dionne Warwick** revolutionized soul music along with countless other vocalists.

In 1959, Berry Gordy founded Motown Records, which eventually made it possible for many more Black singers and groups to be heard and become popular in the United States. Their roster of recording stars included The Miracles, **Martha and the Vandellas**, Marvin Gaye, The Temptations, **The Supremes**, and many others. It was the first time a recording studio had set out to achieve mainstream success with a roster of all-Black recording artists.

In the 1970s, Black vocalists such as **Gloria Gaynor**, **Thelma Houston**, **Vicki Sue Robinson**, and **Donna Summer**, along with others, helped popularize disco music.

In the 1980s, Michael Jackson recorded *Thriller*, the greatest selling record of all time. The album had an enormous influence on Black musicians, and the 1980s saw a whole slew of vocalists crossing over into mainstream success, including **Tina Turner**, Lionel Ritchie, Luther Vandross, **Whitney Houston**, and **Janet Jackson**.

During the 1980s, rap and hip-hop hit the mainstream as well, and recording artists such as **MC Lyte**, **Queen Latifah**, **Monie Love**, and **Salt-N-Pepa** shot up the charts.

In the 1990s, singing groups whose roots were in soul music emerged, like New Edition, Boyz II Men, Jodeci, Dru Hill, Blackstreet, and Jagged Edge. Girl groups became popular as well with the ascent of **TLC**, **Destiny's Child**, **SWV**, and **En Vogue**. Singer-songwriters were also very popular during the 1990s, and **Mariah Carey**, Montell Jordan, **Aaliyah**, and Raphael Saadiq all came to fame during that time.

JACKIE /HANE:
Free At Last

Jackie Shane was a pioneering transgender rhythm and blues singer who gained popularity in Canada in the 1960s and 1970s. Born in 1940 in Nashville, Tennessee, Shane began performing in women's clothing in the 1950s. She left the Jim Crow South as soon as she possibly could, taking off for Canada with a traveling carnival in 1959. Shane said of the experience of arriving in Cornwall, Ontario, "I felt free for the first time." She began performing in clubs across Canada and became known for her extravagantly colorful stage performances. Shane had a top ten hit in Canada with "Any Other Way" in 1962. She continued recording and touring across Canada until the 1970s, when she retired from music.

> ### Black Nightingales:
> ### Some Singers You Should Know

Cynthia Erivo is an English actress, singer, and songwriter who has appeared in television shows such as *Chewing Gum* and *The Tunnel*. She first took on a musical role in *Was Looking at the Ceiling and Then I Saw the Sky*. She starred on Broadway in *The Color Purple* in the role of Celie Harris. She won an Emmy for her part in a performance on *The Today Show* with the cast of *The Color Purple*. In

2019, she played Harriet Tubman in the film *Harriet* and was nominated for a Golden Globe Award for her performance. She also earned two Oscar nominations, one for her performance in *Harriet,* the other for best original song for "Stand Up." Erivo is due to play the blue fairy in Disney's live-action remake of the film *Pinocchio,* as well as Elphaba in the film adaptation of *Wicked.*

H.E.R., an acronym for "Having Everything Revealed," is the professional name of Gabriella Sarmiento Wilson, an American singer and songwriter born to a Black father and a Filipina mother. She made her acting debut at the age of nine when she starred in the Nickelodeon TV movie *School Gyrls.* She went on to win Best R&B Performance and Best R&B Album at the 2019 Grammy Awards a decade later for her compilation album *H.E.R.* In 2021, she won the Grammy for Song of the Year for the song "I Can't Breathe." That same year, she won an Academy Award for Best Original Song for "Fight for You" from the movie *Judas and the Black Messiah.*

Lauryn Hill is an American singer, songwriter, rapper, actress, and record producer who created memorable music both with the brilliant hip-hop and neosoul group The Fugees and as a solo artist. In 1999, she was the first woman ever to win five Grammys in one year. Despite the beckoning promise of further commercial success, Hill did what was best for her artistic, spiritual, and mental well-being by quietly leaving the entertainment industry. She was born in 1975 in Newark, New Jersey, and raised in South Orange, New Jersey. When she was growing up, there was always music in her home; her father sang in nightclubs and performed at weddings, and her mother played the piano.

In middle school, once when young Lauryn sang "The Star-Spangled Banner" before a basketball game, her rendition was so well received that a recorded version of it was played before basketball games afterward. While she was still just a freshman in high school, she joined her first musical group, which would later become The Fugees. As a teenager, Hill took acting lessons and even made an appearance on the TV soap opera *As the World Turns*; a couple of years later, she played the role of Rita Louise Watson in the movie *Sister Act* with Whoopi Goldberg. She recorded several bestselling albums with The Fugees, including the group's second album, *The Score*, which reached number one on the *Billboard 200* chart and stayed in the top ten for more than six months, as well as ultimately selling more than 22 million copies worldwide. Her solo album *The Miseducation of Lauryn Hill* debuted at number one on the *Hot Billboard 200* chart and sold approximately ten million copies. This solo opus earned her five Grammy Awards, including wins for Album of the Year and Best New Artist. In all, Lauryn Hill has earned eight Grammy Awards, the most for any female rapper to date. She has said, "We can't plan life. All we can do is be available for it."

Nina Simone was an American singer, songwriter, musician, arranger, and civil rights activist. She was born in 1933 in Tryon, North Carolina, the sixth of eight children in a poor family. She began playing piano at the age of three or four and performed at her local church. She performed at her first concert recital when she was twelve years old. Her music teacher helped Simone by setting up a fund to help pay for her education, and she was able to attend the Allen High School for Girls in Asheville, North Carolina. After she graduated from high school as class valedictorian, her family moved to Philadelphia because she planned to study at the Curtis Institute of Music in Philadelphia.

Simone spent some time studying at Juilliard in New York City before applying to the Curtis Institute, but her hopes for an education in the arts were dashed when that estimable music school rejected her application. She found work as a photographer's assistant and taught piano from her home to help fund private piano lessons with one of the professors from the Curtis Institute, and also began playing at nightclubs to help to further defray expenses. Word soon spread about Simone's talent, and she developed a fan base. She scored a hit in 1958 with her rendition of "I Loves You, Porgy" from the musical *Porgy and Bess*. She then recorded her debut album *Little Girl Blue* in 1959. Following its success, she recorded a number of records over the next few years and began playing in clubs in New York City's Greenwich Village. Eventually, Nina Simone played her music all over the world. In 1964, she began recording and performing protest songs to address racial inequality. She also spoke and performed at civil rights protests and marches throughout the 1960s and early 1970s. In 1993, Simone settled in southern France, where she died in 2003. As she said, "There's no excuse for the young people not knowing who the heroes and heroines are or were."

> **"You've got to learn to leave the table when love's no longer being served."**
>
> **—Nina Simone,**
> civil rights activist as well as famed American
> singer, songwriter, musician, and arranger who
> could play anything by ear. After the Alabama
> church bombing in 1963, she realized she could
> use her music to protest in a way that couldn't
> go unseen or unheard.

Rhythm and blues and country singer **Linda Martell** was the first Black woman to play the Grand Ole Opry at the Ryman Auditorium in Nashville, Tennessee. She was the first Black female country recording artist to gain popularity and hit the charts. In 1969, she became the first Black woman country singer to appear on the highly rated country music TV variety show *Hee Haw*. Her career was short-lived, primarily due to the racist attacks she often suffered while performing in front of white audiences and difficulties with management at her record company; the company's name was Plantation Records, which Martell felt signaled their belief that the Black acts the company signed still belonged down on the plantation. She continued to play music up until 1990 but had to moonlight as a bus driver and an educator to support herself at times when her career as a country musician didn't pay the bills.

MARIAN ANDERSON:
Operatic Talent

Marian Anderson became the first Black woman to perform with the New York Metropolitan Opera; at the invitation of Franklin Delano Roosevelt, she was also the first to perform at the White House. Anderson's father died when she was only twelve years old, leaving her mother to raise her and her siblings alone in Philadelphia. With no extra money to pay for formal lessons, Anderson was largely self-taught and practiced soprano, tenor, alto, and bass parts for her church choir. Impressed by her vocal range and dedication to singing, members of the congregation raised five hundred dollars to pay for formal lessons, and that's all it took for Anderson to gain recognition for her talent. Soon, she was performing at the Lincoln Memorial and Carnegie Hall and gaining fans on both sides of the Atlantic. She sang the national anthem at John F. Kennedy's inauguration and was later awarded the Presidential Medal of Freedom by President Kennedy.

GERTRUDE "MA" RAINEY:

Mother of the Blues

Gertrude "Ma" Rainey was a pioneering blues performer born in 1886. In a small Missouri town in 1902, Ma heard the music that would later become the blues; she was hooked. She began performing the soulful music wherever she went, touring with various jazz combos and jug bands throughout the South. Rainey was rare among singers of the day in that she wrote fully one in three of her songs herself. In 1923, she made her first album for the Paramount Company. Over the next five years, she recorded ninety-two songs, including "See See Rider," "Prove It on Me," "Blues Oh Blues," "Sleep Talking," "Oh Papa Blues," "Trust No Man," "Slave to the Blues," "New Bo-Weavil Blues," and "Slow Driving Moan." These, along with a few tracks recorded the next year with a young session player named Louis Armstrong, ended up being the only recordings of her voice to endure past her lifetime. She continued to perform well into the 1930s, influencing the blues genre with her deep contralto voice; no wonder she was known as the "mother of the blues." Ma Rainey was inducted into the Blues Hall of Fame in 1983 and the Rock and Roll Hall of Fame in 1990.

BE//IE /MITH:
Empress of the Blues

Bessie Smith was the most popular blues singer of the 1920s and 1930s, and one of the most influential ever. She was born in 1894 in Chattanooga, Tennessee. Her parents and a brother died when she was very young, and Smith and her surviving brother supported themselves by busking on the streets of Chattanooga. Smith sang and danced while her brother played guitar, often for pennies. Due to the extreme poverty in which she grew up, Smith never received a formal education.

Her older brother Clarence joined a traveling troupe owned by a man named Moses Stokes and then left town without telling Smith. When he returned to Chattanooga with the Stokes troupe in 1912, he arranged for the eighteen-year-old Smith to audition for a spot in the troupe. At the time, Ma Rainey was performing with them as a singer, so Smith was hired on to dance. Eventually, Smith moved up within the troupe to the chorus line and then began booking gigs on the Black-owned Theater Owners Booking Association (TOBA) circuit. She began forming her own act around 1913, making the Atlanta nightclub "81" her home base. She started to gain a reputation in the South and up along the East Coast for her talent. In 1923, she signed a recording contract with Columbia Records. When Columbia issued a "race records" series, Smith's recording of "Cemetery Blues" was the first they released. Both the A-side and B-side songs on her first record, "Downhearted Blues" backed by "Gulf Coast Blues," became hits, and Smith's career took off as she became the top headliner on the TOBA circuit.

Smith's sound wasn't everyone's cup of tea, however. She was considered "rough" by many, and her tolerant attitudes about sexual freedom didn't sit well with the popular morality of the time. However, despite anyone's objections to her, she was the highest paid blues performer of the 1920s, traveling to her concert gigs in her own seventy-two-foot railroad car that she purchased with her own money. Smith made 160 recordings for Columbia, often accompanied by the most popular musicians of the era, including Louis Armstrong, Coleman Hawkins, Fletcher Henderson, James P. Johnson, Joe Smith, and Charlie Green. She had a string of hit records. Her recording career was cut short by the Great Depression, which had a devastating impact on the music industry, as did the end of the vaudeville era. Smith continued to perform at nightclubs and even appeared on Broadway. She died at the age of forty-three following an automobile accident; the world lost "the Empress of the Blues" far too soon.

BILLIE HOLIDAY:
Lady Day

Nicknamed "Lady Day," **Billie Holiday** was an American jazz and swing singer who revolutionized both genres and had a lasting impact on myriad styles of music that is felt to this day. Born in 1915 in Philadelphia, Pennsylvania, Holiday had a rough childhood. Her mother had become pregnant as an unwed teen, and Billie's father left soon after she was born. Her mother's parents threw her out of the house for becoming pregnant and arranged for an older half-sister to raise her in Baltimore.

Frequently truant as a young girl, Holiday was sent to a Catholic Reform School called the House of the Good Shepherd when she was nine years old. During her nine months in the reform school, her mother opened a restaurant, and Holiday was paroled to her. She and her mother worked long hours at the restaurant. When she was eleven, her mother discovered an adult male neighbor trying to rape Holiday. she was taken into protective custody as a material witness in the rape case against the neighbor, and remained under lock and key as a witness at the House of the Good Shepherd until she was twelve. Upon her release, Holiday found work in a brothel as an errand girl for the prostitutes who lived there and their madam, as well as scrubbing floors and marble steps for people in her neighborhood. When her mother moved to Harlem, Holiday followed her a year later. She began singing in nightclubs in Harlem as a young teenager and soon gained a following.

In 1933, at the age of eighteen, she met producer John Hammond, who arranged for her first recordings with Benny Goodman. She recorded two songs: "Your Mother's Son-In-Law" and "Riffin' the Scotch," the latter of which became her first hit. From 1935–1941, Holiday's career took off and she recorded a string of hits with pianist/arranger Teddy Wilson. She toured with Count Basie's orchestra in 1937, and in 1938, she made history when Artie Shaw invited her to front his famous orchestra, the first time a Black woman appeared with a white band. In the 1930s, Holiday was introduced to "Strange Fruit," a poignant anti-racist poem by second generation Russian Jewish immigrant songwriter Abel Meerapol. The haunting music that accompanied the poem was written especially for her with Holiday as a cowriter, resulting in a song noted by many music critics as the first civil rights protest song. When Holiday's recording studio refused to record it, she went to Commodore Records, an independent recording studio where she could record whatever she wanted. "Strange Fruit" became an instant hit and sparked a cultural revolution with its vivid depiction of a lynching. In 1939, she wrote "God Bless the Child" with Arthur Herzog. The song has become part of the jazz lexicon, and Holiday's recording of it was yet another hit for her.

In the 1950s, Holiday made over 100 recordings, including "Lady Sings the Blues." She toured Europe, where she was a sensation. Her music shaped not only jazz and swing, but the blues, soul, and rock and roll. She continues to be cited as an influence by many recording artists today. Holiday died at the age of forty-four from cirrhosis of the liver in 1959, but "Lady Day," the nickname fellow musician Lester Young gave her, will forever be remembered as one of the greatest jazz vocalists of all time.

VINNETTE JUSTINE CARROLL:
First to Direct on Broadway

Vinnette Justine Carroll became the first Black American woman Broadway director when she helmed the 1972 musical *Don't Bother Me, I Can't Cope*. She was also the first Black woman to earn a Tony Award nomination for directing that musical and remained the only Black woman nominated for a Tony for stage direction until 2016.

Black women singers have become even more popular in recent years. Topping the charts, these chanteuses have revolutionized the music industry. Legend **Diana Ross** continues to perform, with a career spanning over six decades. **Janet Jackson** has been singing since she was a little girl and has sold over 100 million records worldwide. Afro-Cuban singer **Celia Cruz**, who supposedly started singing in 1926 at only nine months old, went on to become the "Queen of Salsa Music" with a career lasting more than sixty years. Through her outspoken voice, her presence, and her beautiful dark skin, she has made space for Afro-Latinos to pridefully embrace their diverse and beautiful lineage. When actor and vocalist **Amandla Stenberg** is not busy singing their heart out with their band HoneyWater, they use their platform to help teens cope with anxiety as well as to call out multibillionaires for cultural appropriation. Having been snubbed by the Grammys in the early 2000s despite no fewer than seven nominations, **India Arie,** defying that disappointment, has continued writing and recording music from her heart, winning two Grammy Awards for her second album the next year. Trinidadian American singer, songwriter, actress, and model **Nicki Minaj** uses her music as activism to empower women to be who they want to be. She dropped out of a concert in Saudi Arabia after a well-known women's rights activist was arrested.

Big Mama Thornton was an American rhythm and blues singer and songwriter. Her family in Alabama was musical by nature, and she began singing in church as a young girl. In 1940, she left home and joined Sammy Green's Hot Harlem Revue, where she was billed as "the new Bessie Smith." In 1951, she signed a recording contract with Peacock Records and performed at the Apollo Theater in Harlem. In 1952, she recorded "Hound Dog;" the recording topped the charts, selling more than half a million copies. The song later became a hit for Elvis Presley, but Big Mama's recording helped usher in the era of rock and roll. She also recorded the song "Ball and Chain," which was later covered by Janis Joplin.

As the blues, rhythm and blues, and jazz genres were being popularized by notable Black women singers, meanwhile, in Hollywood, Black actresses were beginning to become popular on television and in the movies.

Black Actresses Make Herstory

Born in 1896, singer and actress **Ethel Waters** was a trailblazer in the entertainment industry. She was the first Black actress to appear on Broadway, as well as only the second Black actor to receive an Academy Award nomination, and the first Black person, female or male, to be featured in her own television show, *The Ethel Waters Show*, which aired a decade before Nat King Cole's popular evening show.

In 1939, **Hattie McDaniel** made history when she brought home an Academy Award for Best Supporting Actress in *Gone with the Wind*, the first Black actor ever to win an Oscar. She was also the first Black American woman to sing on the radio in the United States and has not one but *two* stars on the Hollywood Walk of Fame.

"Moms" Mabley, born Loretta Mary Aiken in 1894, was a comedic genius who after starting her performing career in the late years of the vaudeville circuit, went on to be the first Black woman comedian in America to bring her brilliant stand-up act to national television, appearing several times on *The Smothers Brothers Comedy Hour*. She was also the very first female entertainer to perform stand-up as a solo act at Harlem's noted Apollo Theater.

LENA HORNE:
Legendary Talent

Lena Horne was an American dancer, actress, and Grammy-winning singer as well as a civil rights activist. Her career spanned more than seventy years, and she was a trailblazer in many ways. When she was sixteen, she dropped out of high school and joined the chorus of the Cotton Club in Harlem; within a year, she had a featured role in the Cotton Club Parade. She made her Broadway debut in the 1934 opening run of the play *Dance with Your Gods*. She later sang for a time with Noble Sisso & His Orchestra, and then appeared in the musical revue *Lew Leslie's Blackbirds of 1939*, also on Broadway. She then joined a well-known white swing band, the Charlie Barnet Orchestra. Barnet was one of the first to integrate his band, but Horne still faced discrimination and could not socialize or even stay in the segregated lodgings booked for the group by many of the venues where the band performed. She left the tour rather than suffer the indignity of being treated so poorly. She returned to New York, where she performed at the Café Society nightclub, a venue that was popular with both white and Black music lovers.

After a long stint at the Savoy nightclub, Horne's career got a boost when she was featured in *Life* magazine. She became the highest paid Black entertainer of her time and signed a seven-year contract with MGM. One stipulation of her contract made sure that Horne would not be relegated to playing domestic servants in her film roles, which was standard treatment in the industry for Black entertainers of the era. Horne was placed in several films, mostly in chorus roles that could easily be edited out for Southern audiences, but she landed two lead roles in *Cabin in the Sky* and *Stormy Weather*. The title song for *Stormy Weather* became a signature favorite of hers, one that she continued to sing for decades to audiences all around the world. She also starred in the 1969 western *Death of a Gunfighter*.

Her final film role was in 1978, in *The Wiz*, an adaptation of *The Wizard of Oz* that featured an all-Black cast that also included Diana Ross and Michael Jackson. Horne played Glinda, the Good Witch of the North. By the end of the 1940s, Horne had filed suit against several clubs for discrimination and had also joined a leftist group, Progressive Citizens of America. Exercising her freedom of political association and expression in McCarthy-era America brought persecution, and Horne soon found herself blacklisted. While she was able to find work at nightclubs and in Europe, she had trouble finding work in film and went more than a decade without any major roles until the blacklist was ended. Instead, Horne's singing career took off, and she made several popular albums including *It's Love* (1955) and *Stormy Weather* (1957).

Her live album, *Lena Horne at the Waldorf Astoria*, became the biggest selling album by any woman at the time for

RCA. Horne was very active in the American Civil Rights Movement. She performed at rallies around the country representing the National Association for the Advancement of Colored People (NAACP) and the National Council for Negro Women. She also participated in the 1963 March on Washington. She retired from performing in 1980 but returned to the stage in 1981 in a one-woman show, *Lena Horne: The Lady and Her Music*. The show ran on Broadway for fourteen months, then toured in the United States and overseas. It won a Drama Desk Award, a special Tony, and two Grammys for its soundtrack.

While Lena Horne was rising to fame, elsewhere in the world of entertainment, other Black women were bringing their talents to both the small and the big screens.

In 1953, **Dorothy Dandridge** was the first Black woman to appear on the cover of *Life* magazine; she played a leading role in *Carmen Jones*, a film with an all-Black cast directed by Otto Preminger. The following year, Dandridge became the first Black American to earn an Academy Award nomination for best actress.

Carmen Jones also launched the career of Golden Globe Award winner **Diahann Carroll**, who had performed on Broadway prior to the film. Carroll became the first Black actress to land a leading role in any television series when she became the star of the popular drama series *Julia*. Her role in *Julia* was notable because it was one of the first television roles featuring a Black actress who wasn't cast as a domestic worker in a white household.

In 1957, *The Nat King Cole Show* debuted on television, and Americans began to see more Black actors and actresses on their television screens. Nat King Cole hosted stars like Ella Fitzgerald, Eartha Kitt, and Mahalia Jackson.

ELLA FITZGERALD:
First Lady of Jazz

Ella Fitzgerald was an American jazz singer. She was born in 1917 in Newport News, Virginia. Her parents broke up when she was very young, and she moved with her mother to Yonkers, New York, where they lived with her mother's longtime boyfriend. As a child, Fitzgerald often took on odd jobs to help support her family. Their home was in a mixed-race neighborhood. Fitzgerald used to catch the train to Harlem to watch acts at the Apollo Theater. After her mother died in 1932 from injuries she received in a car accident, Fitzgerald moved to Harlem to live with an aunt. Fitzgerald wasn't happy in Harlem; she began skipping school, and her grades began to drop. She got in trouble with the police and was sent to a girls' reform school, where she was beaten. Once out of the reform school, Fitzgerald found herself alone and broke in Harlem during the Great Depression. In 1934, she won the opportunity to perform in a talent contest at the Apollo Theater, in which she won first place! After that, she entered as many talent contests as she could. Eventually, Fitzgerald became the most popular jazz singer in America and went on to win thirteen Grammy Awards and sell over 40 million albums. She toured all over the world performing for mixed audiences. Her manager insisted that Fitzgerald and her band be treated equally and refused to allow any kind of discrimination when they were touring, even in the Deep South. Fitzgerald died in 1966 after a few years of diabetic complications, but she left an enduring legacy in the world of music.

EARTHA KITT:
The Most Exciting Woman in the World

Eartha Kitt, the woman Orson Welles once called "the most exciting woman in the world," came into this world on a cotton plantation in South Carolina, but the vicissitudes of her family life brought her to Harlem, where she attended high school. On a friend's dare, Kitt tried out for the Katherine Dunham Dance Company while still a teenager and won a spot as a dancer and singer. She toured worldwide with the dance company and was spotted by a Paris nightclub owner, who booked her as a featured singer. Her unique charm and personality quickly gained her fame. In New York, she performed on Broadway and began to be signed for film roles and recording contracts. During her early years in show business, she published her first autobiography, *Thursday's Child*. She could sing in ten languages and toured in over one hundred countries. In 1967, she played Catwoman on the television series *Batman*, a role in which she was an instant sensation.

But in 1968, while at a luncheon at the White House hosted by Lady Bird Johnson, Kitt spoke out against the Vietnam War and was then blacklisted in the United States, where no one would hire her to perform from that point on. She was forced to live overseas for many years. In 1974, she returned to the United States for an acclaimed Carnegie Hall concert. She published three more books and earned Tony and Grammy nominations for her performing arts work. Kitt was also a busy activist: She founded the Kittsville Youth Foundation, which helped underprivileged children in the Watts section of Los Angeles. She was an anti-war activist and used her platform as a performing artist to speak out against the war in Vietnam, as well as supporting LGBTQ+ rights, including marriage equality.

Black actresses have won accolades throughout history, and they deserve full public acknowledgment of their talents. In 1961, a screen adaptation of Lorraine Hansberry's *A Raisin in the Sun* launched the career of **Ruby Dee**, who became the first Black actress to play a feature role on a prime-time TV show. **Phylicia Rashad**, who garnered popularity in her role as Clair Huxtable on *The Cosby Show*, was the first Black actress to win a Tony Award for Best

Performance by a Leading Actress in a Play for her role in the remake of Lorraine Hansberry's *A Raisin in the Sun*.

As Black actresses began to demand more challenging roles, more roles playing dynamic characters who defied stereotypes became available to them. **Trina Parks** starred in 1971's *Diamonds are Forever* as Thumper, the first ever Black James Bond girl. A talented singer and dancer as well as actress, Parks also helped to choreograph the Tony Award-winning Broadway musical, *The Wiz*. Following Trina Parks's turn as James Bond's badass nemesis, **Gloria Hendry** played Bond girl Rosie Carver in *Live and Let Die* in 1973. Hendry was the first Black actress to portray a Bond love interest. When the film aired in South Africa, which was still under apartheid at the time, all the love scenes between Parks and Roger Moore were edited out of the film.

Gail Fisher was an actress known for the firsts she accomplished in a number of key areas of the entertainment industry. She is primarily known for her role as Peggy Fair on the detective series *Mannix*, which aired from 1968–1975. Fisher won two Golden Globe Awards and an Emmy Award for her work on the series—the first Black actress to win either award. She also won an NAACP Image Award in 1969. Fisher had a long career spanning three decades; after *Mannix* was canceled in 1975, she went on to guest star on many other television shows for the next twenty-five years.

Halle Berry is the first and only Black actress to date to have received the Academy Award for Best Actress. She won her breakthrough Oscar in 2002 for her performance in the film *Monster's Ball*; as she accepted her award, she acknowledged the work of earlier Black actresses who served as role models to those who followed, as well as some actresses who were still rising to fame at the time. Among the actresses to whom she directed accolades were Dorothy Dandridge, Lena Horne, and Jada Pinkett Smith. During her speech, Berry directly addressed the lack of representation of women of color in the Academy's history by stating that her award was dedicated to "every nameless, faceless woman of color who now has a chance because this door tonight has been opened."

In 2017, American actress **Zendaya** had her film breakthrough with the Marvel Cinematic Universe film *Spiderman: Homecoming*. That same year, she starred in *The Greatest Showman*; her song "Rewrite the Stars" from the musical went double platinum. In addition to singing, acting, and dancing, Zendaya is an ambassador for Convoy of Hope.

She celebrated her eighteenth birthday with a campaign to help feed at least 150 hungry children in Haiti, Tanzania, and the Philippines, and she celebrated her twentieth birthday by raising $50,000 to support a women's empowerment initiative. She has her own clothing line, and has written a book, *Between U and Me: How to Rock Your Tween Years with Style and Confidence.*

Black actresses persevere. American actress, humorist, and singer **Pearl Bailey** received her degree in theology at the age of sixty-seven, proving it's never too late to go after what you want. Actress and author **Lupita Nyong'o** is the first Mexican and first Kenyan ever to win an Oscar. She was at one point close to giving up on her acting career, but she decided her dream of acting couldn't be denied. Now, she inspires millions of young Black girls to chase their dreams and realize their talents.

Black actresses embrace worthy causes: **Jada Pinkett Smith** uses her show *Red Table Talk* to highlight people whose stories inspire healing change. **Taraji P. Henson** has also brought awareness to the importance of maintaining mental health through her foundation, the Boris Lawrence Henson Foundation, with the aim of offering culturally competent therapy to those with limited access.

Black actresses have high expectations of themselves. **Viola Davis** has won Tony, Oscar, and Emmy Awards, a well-deserved trifecta; it has been noted that she brings a focused precision to each role she embodies. Actress **Cicely Tyson** won many awards and also chose not to take roles that depicted Black women in a negative light. **Quvenzhané**

Wallis made history as the youngest actress ever to receive a nomination for an Oscar for Best Actress for her role as Hushpuppy in *Beasts of the Southern Wild*. She also made history when she became the first Black actress to play the lead role in *Annie* in the 2014 motion picture remake. **Anika Noni Rose**, a film and Broadway actress, was the voice actress behind Princess Tiana, Disney's first Black animated princess, in *The Princess and the Frog*. **Samira Wiley** is an actress and producer known for *Orange Is the New Black* (2013), *The Sitter* (2011), and *The Handmaid's Tale* (2017).

Small-screen outlets like HBO and Netflix are writing film scripts like *Treme* and *Underground Railroad* that feature strong roles for Black actresses. There's a new generation of talented Black directors and producers ready to make their mark in Hollywood, and Black-produced films are generating more ticket sales than ever. Showrunner **Shonda Rhimes**, best known for the television drama *Grey's Anatomy*, became the first woman to create three hit shows with more than a hundred episodes each. **Issa Rae** became the first Black woman to create and star in a premium cable series: She is the creator and star of HBO's hit series, *Insecure*. **Ava DuVernay** became the first Black woman to direct a film nominated for a Best Picture Oscar– *Selma*. She also became the first Black female director to win the director's prize at the Sundance Film Festival in 2012. **Darnell Martin** was the first Black American woman to direct a major studio movie when she directed Columbia Pictures' *I Like It Like That*. In the streaming age, **Quinta Brunson** is reviving the network sitcom with her hit show *Abbott Elementary*, which she created and stars in.

STORM REID:
Taking the World by Storm

Up-and-coming actress **Storm Reid** was certain of her future in acting at a very young age; at age nine, she convinced her parents to move the family to Los Angeles so she could pursue a career in film and television. A string of small roles eventually led to her film debut in 2013's *12 Years a Slave*, released when Reid was all of ten years old. This performance was followed by an appearance in the superhero movie *Sleight,* and then her breakout: Disney's adaptation of the classic children's science fiction novel *A Wrinkle in Time*. She also made numerous appearances on television, including on *NCIS: Los Angeles* and *Chicago P.D.* She has acted in roles on the HBO series *Euphoria* and the Netflix series *Central Park.* In an interview with *The Washington Post*, she said that her main goal was to "represent girls who look like me and let them know they can do anything."

**"I'm gonna take this world by storm.
Pun intended."**

—Storm Reid

EVELYN PREER:
First Lady of the Screen

Evelyn Preer, an actress and vocalist, was the first Black actress to rise to fame in the early twentieth century. She broke boundaries limiting Black actresses of the time, who were often relegated to playing domestic servants or other stereotyped roles. Instead of being pigeonholed in such roles, Preer acted in plays by canonical and iconic playwrights like Oscar Wilde and William Shakespeare and went on to star in many films beginning in 1919. In addition to her acting career, she was a jazz singer of note during the very beginnings of the musical style, recording with artists like Duke Ellington.

Black women have changed the way we experience entertainment. They built their careers in an atmosphere that was frequently unwelcoming to Black women and defied the expectations Hollywood and the world of music held for them, blazing new trails to stardom. Along the way, they fought for equality, standing shoulder to shoulder with civil rights icons.

Some Black women blazed their own trails in unexpected ways, like **Katherine Dunham**, both an anthropologist and a choreographer who lived among the Jamaican Accompong people in 1935, conducting research on the African roots of their diasporic culture and how they incorporated these traditions into interpretive and preservationist dance.

The fearless creativity of these sheroes and their relentless pursuit of artistic truth have freed the human imagination, allowing it to expand to its limitless bounds. They have produced art that shocks and poetry that pierces, created new ritual dances, designed fantastic fashions, and looked into the very heart of the darkness that is the feminine. The lives of these women suggest that real inspiration can come only from being true to yourself at any cost.

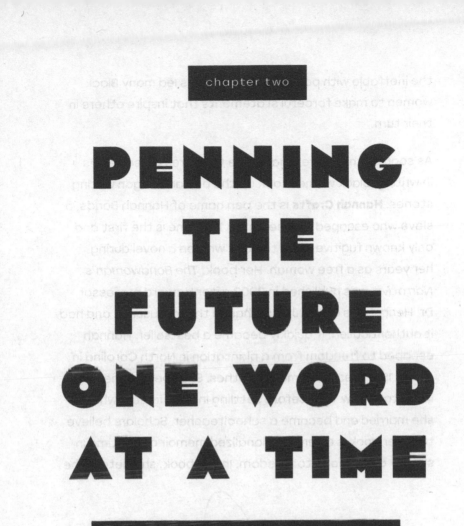

chapter two

PENNING THE FUTURE ONE WORD AT A TIME

AWESOME BLACK WOMEN WRITERS

Women who create have the advantage when it comes to inspiration, no doubt about it. Before penning a poem or mustering a masterpiece, Black women have no need to invoke any semi-divine beings to give them a good idea. Black women embody their own muse. Tapping this inner resource has unleashed an artistry that has changed the world many times over. The impulse to express the ineffable with poetry and fiction has led many Black women to make forceful statements that inspire others in their turn.

As soon as they were legally able to express themselves in writing, Black women took up the pen and began writing stories. **Hannah Crafts** is the pen name of Hannah Bonds, a slave who escaped to freedom in 1857. She is the first and only known fugitive slave to have written a novel during her years as a free woman. Her book, *The Bondwoman's Narrative*, was published in 2002 after Harvard professor Dr. Henry Louis Gates Jr. purchased the manuscript and had it authenticated. It quickly became a bestseller. Hannah escaped to freedom from a plantation in North Carolina in about 1857 dressed in men's clothes. She spent some time in upstate New York before settling in New Jersey, where she married and became a schoolteacher. Scholars believe that her book is a semi-fictionalized memoir of her time in slavery and escape to freedom. In the book, she details the intimate lives of her owner, a minister to Nicaragua, and his family.

Black women are active elsewhere in the fields of nonfiction and journalism. **Nancy Hicks Maynard** became the first Black American woman reporter hired by *The New York Times*. She was also the first Black woman to own a newspaper (with her husband) with her purchase of the *Oakland Tribune* in 1983.

Black women weave a rich tapestry of experience into their writing. They blend the experience of being Black in a white world into the weave and build worlds with rich characters and settings. They challenge the canon of "acceptable" literature and bring to life stories that would remain untold without their voices recording for posterity what they have observed.

TONI MORRISON:
The Truest Eye

Toni Morrison comes from small-town, working-class Ohio, a state that fell "between" on the Civil War issue of slavery, a state with many stops along the Underground Railroad, and a state where many crosses burned "neither plantation nor ghetto." She has made this her canvas for her rich, original stories that dare tell uncomfortable truths. And for her daring, she won the Nobel Prize in Literature.

Born in 1931 as Chloe Anthony Wofford, young Toni and her parents worked hard as sharecroppers in their adopted northern home of Lorain, Ohio. She was keenly interested in language as a child and loved hearing ghost stories, songs, and thundering sermons at church. After high school, she attended Howard University and graduated at the age of twenty-two, following that with a master's program at Cornell. Her thesis paper examined the theme of suicide in the works of Virginia Woolf and William Faulkner. She began teaching at Howard and met and married a Jamaican architect, Harold Morrison, with whom she had two sons, Harold Ford and Slade. The marriage was short-lived, and she took the children and moved to Syracuse, and then later to New York City, where she was hired by Random House as senior editor. Morrison worked on several major Black autobiographies of the time, including those of Black Power revolutionary Angela Davis and world champion boxer Muhammed Ali.

As a writer, Toni Morrison made an immediate mark upon America's literary landscape with *The Bluest Eye*, published in 1970, and *Sula*, published three years later. Her next book, *Song of Solomon*, won the National Book Critics' Circle Award in 1978. In 1983, she left Random House to devote herself full-time to writing and spent the next five years writing *Beloved*, the fantastical and tragic story of ex-slave Sethe and her children.

Her writing focused on Black women who had previously been ignored. Her lyrical language combines with both realistic and mythic plot elements to create a distinctive style all her own. In 1993, Morrison won the Nobel Prize in

Literature, the first Black American to do so. She said, "I am outrageously happy. But what is most wonderful for me personally is to know that the prize has been awarded to an African American. Winning as an American is very special—but winning as a Black American is a knockout."

> **"Had I loved the life that the state planned for me from the beginning, I would have lived and died in somebody else's kitchen."**
>
> **—Toni Morrison,**
> in a speech to the International Literary Congress in New York

ZORA NEALE HUR/TON:
Seraph of the Sun

Zora Neale Hurston's readership is much larger now than it was at the height of her career. More than half a century after her death in 1960, her body of work has been reprinted hundreds of times, ensuring her legacy in our literary heritage. A writer of the Harlem Renaissance, Hurston spoke for the silenced—Black women. Her work, which includes five novels, more than fifty short stories and essays, a short story collection, and her autobiography, demonstrates her commitment to the culture of her people and her anthropological scholarship of Black language and history.

Born in rural Florida in 1891, Hurston was very outspoken, insisting upon equality and eschewing the traditional roles of a Black woman of her day. For this, she credits her precious mother, Lucy, who urged her to "jump at de sun!" when she was nine. Despite a bumpy childhood with a stepmother she didn't care for, Hurston thrived in the all-Black town of Eatonville, where she saw a real-life example of peaceful and good government by and for Black people. Her father, a popular Baptist preacher who was elected and served as mayor of the town several times, warned his daughter that the world outside would be vastly different. She bounced among various relatives until, at fourteen, she headed out to make her own way in the world, working as a maid for a group of Gilbert and Sullivan traveling players. Landing in New York City, Hurston made some fateful connections with leaders of the Harlem Renaissance, including Langston Hughes, Alan Locke, and Montgomery Gregory.

With the help of financial aid, Hurston received an excellent education at Barnard College in New York City, where she was mentored by Franz Boas, the leading anthropologist of the day who also had mentored Margaret Mead. Boas saw Hurston's endless drive and curiosity and set her to the task of gathering the cultural history of her people. After graduation, Hurston returned to Florida to record Black folklore. She married a man she met there,

Herbert Sheen, but divorced not long after, one of three divorces in her lifetime. In 1934, she was the recipient of a fellowship to collect more folklore and went on a quest for knowledge about her people that took her to New Orleans, Jamaica, Haiti, and the Bahamas, where she studied voodoo in addition to her usual linguistics and tall stories. The data she aggregated on this epic trip constituted the foundations for *Mules and Men* and *Tell My Horse*. *Jonah's Gourd Vine* is regarded as one of her finest works of fiction, and *Their Eyes Were Watching God* is hailed as her masterpiece. One of Hurston's greatest proponents, novelist Alice Walker, offers a powerful endorsement of Hurston's opus, "There is no book more important to me than this one."

Unfortunately, her friendship with Langston Hughes broke down over a play on which they collaborated, *Mule Bone*. The forties saw a further decline of Zora Neale Hurston's career. Her essay "How it Feels to be Colored Me" drew fire for its inflammatory frankness regarding what Hurston saw as the wholly unfair system of Jim Crow injustice. In 1940s America, Hurston's literary protests fell on unwilling ears.

In 1948, she was the victim of a trumped-up charge of child molestation in New York City. The case was thrown out, but Hurston, devastated, headed back to Florida. Undaunted, she continued to act from her conscience, protesting 1954's *Brown vs. Topeka Board of Education*, taking the position that it smacked of a bias toward Black students and Southern schools as inferior. Hurston, one of America's most original literary scholars, linguists, mythographers, and novelists, had to work as a librarian, a substitute teacher, and even as a maid to try to pay her bills. She was working on a book and still submitting articles to *The Saturday Evening Post* and *The American Legion Magazine* even in her most desperate of circumstances.

When she died of heart failure in January of 1960, she was penniless and homeless, taking shelter at the Saint Lucie Welfare Home. Hurston's work languished, almost forgotten, until her masterful writing was "rediscovered" in the 1970s. She saw Black culture as a treasure to be celebrated and shared; she saw Caucasian culture as feeble next to the vitality of Black idiom and storytelling. Alice Walker searched out Hurston's unmarked pauper's grave in Fort Pierce, Florida, and wrote about her pilgrimage to find her sheroic fore-sister for *Ms.* magazine in 1975. Her article "In Search of Zora Neale Hurston" created an avalanche of renewed interest in the writer who had been at the very epicenter of the Harlem Renaissance. The gravestone Walker had made following that visit read, "Zora Neal Hurston, A Genius of the South. Novelist, Folklorist, Anthropologist."

> "I was not comfortable to be around. Strange things must have looked out of my eyes like Lazarus after his resurrection...I have been in sorrow's kitchen and licked out all the pots...I have stood on the peaky mountain with a harp and a sword in my hands."
>
> **—Zora Neale Hurston in** ***Dust Tracks on a Road***, her autobiography, in which she predicts her whole life in twelve visions, including her ultimate destitution

HARRIET E. ADAMS WILSON:
Provocateur

Like many other literary women, **Harriet Wilson** was also left out of the history books. She was the first Black woman to publish a novel in English and the first Black person, male or female, to publish a novel in America.

Sadly, we know precious little about this author. Harriet E. Adams Wilson is believed to have been born in Fredericksburg, Virginia, in 1807 or 1808 and trained in millinery as her trade; she was then deserted and left in poverty by her sailor husband, who impregnated her before the abandonment. Her son from this relationship, George Mason Wilson, died at age seven, a year after the publication of the one novel it is known that Wilson wrote.

Her groundbreaking work, *Our Nig*, a title deliberately chosen for its challenge and daring, was printed by George C. Rand and Avery of Boston. It is believed Wilson self-published *Our Nig* to prove a political point, as evidenced by the full title, *Our Nig, or, Sketches from the Life of a Free Black, in A Two-Story White House, North, Showing That Slavery's Shadows Fall Even There*, with the author credit to "Our Nig."

Our Nig was ignored by reviewers and readers and barely sold. Wilson's work was in the dustbin of lost history until Henry Louis Gates Jr. discovered it and reissued it in 1983. Gates observed that the provocative title probably contributed to the novel's near oblivion. The plot, a marriage between a white woman and a Black man, would have alienated many readers of the time.

N.K. JEMISIN:
Next-Generation Nerd Turned Pioneering Prizewinner

Nora K. Jemisin is an award-winning writer of speculative fiction (which includes such genre categories as science fiction and fantasy), including both numerous short stories and eight full-length novels. Born in 1972, she started off her writing career with a splash when *The Hundred Thousand Kingdoms* won the Locus Award for Best First Novel in 2011. That same year, she also cowrote a nonfiction work, *Geek Wisdom: The Sacred Teachings of Nerd Culture*. She was a counseling psychologist and educator with degrees from Tulane and the University of Maryland; but via a 2016 Patreon campaign, she was able to raise enough collective crowdfunding so that since then, she has been able to focus solely on her writing, exploring themes including cultural conflicts and inequality. Also, from 2016 to 2019, "Otherworldly," her column on science fiction, ran in *The New York Times*; she continues to contribute long-form reviews to that flagship newspaper.

She is the author of the Broken Earth trilogy, consisting of *The Fifth Season* (2015), *The Obelisk Gate* (2016), and *The Stone Sky* (2017); when *The Fifth Season* won a Hugo Award for Best Novel, she became the first African American author to win a Hugo in that category. Then each of the two sequels won her Hugo Awards, making her the only author ever to win the Best Novel Hugo in three consecutive years. *The Stone Sky* also won a Nebula Best Novel Award as well as a Locus Best Fantasy Award, and a television adaptation of *The Fifth Season* is planned as of this writing. In 2019, a collection of her short stories entitled *How*

Long 'til Black Future Month? won an American Libraries Association Alex Award. Besides her distinguished fiction career, she is also an anti-racist and feminist political blogger. N.K. Jemisin lives in Brooklyn and is just hitting her stride as a writer of note.

GWENDOLYN BENNETT:
The Ebony Flute

Gwendolyn Bennett, a respected writer and artist, was born in Texas in 1902. Among her many talents, she was a poet, short story writer, columnist, journalist, illustrator, graphic artist, arts educator, teacher, and administrator for the New York City Works Progress Administration Federal Arts Project.

Bennett received her education from Columbia University and the Pratt Institute in New York, as well as at the Académie Julian and the École du Panthéon in Paris. As an artist, she worked with a variety of media, including watercolor, oil, woodcuts, pen and ink, and batik. Her work appeared on the covers of publications such as *The Crisis* and *Opportunity*. She taught design, watercolor painting, and craft classes at Howard University. She was a member of the Harlem Artists Guild in New York. In addition, she was the director of the Harlem Community Arts Center. She served on the board of the Negro Playwright's Guild and helped develop the George Washington Carver Community School. A strong advocate for Black women's rights during the Harlem Renaissance, she pushed literature and education for women.

Her early participation in Harlem literary circles energized the Harlem Renaissance. Poets and writers who like her emphasized racial pride and she had an important influence on the cultural revival of African American music, dance, art, fashion, literature, theatre, politics, and scholarship. As a volunteer at the 135th Street Library in Harlem, she helped organize poetry readings, book discussions, and other cultural activities. Bennett and her librarian friend Regina Anderson are the ones who came up with the idea for the Civic Club Dinner. At one of the dinners hosted by Charles Johnson, Bennett's poem, "To Usward," was selected as the dedication for the introduction of Jessie Fauset's novel *There Is Confusion.*

Throughout her career as a teacher and artist, she was an active participant in the Black arts community. In Harlem, she nurtured the talents of young Black artists and writers through a support group that included such writers as Langston Hughes, Countee Cullen, Eric Walrond, Helene Johnson, Wallace Thurman, Richard Bruce Nugent, Aaron Douglas, Alta Douglass, Rudolph Fisher, and Zora Neale Hurston. The group was designed to encourage these young writers to support one another and to aspire to achieving the level of more established scholars like Charles S. Johnson, Alain Locke, W. E. B. Du Bois, Jessie Fauset, and James Weldon Johnson. In her Harlem literary circles, Bennett created a place for writers to gather, share ideas, and find inspiration.

Many of her poems, short stories, and nonfiction columns appeared in literary journals, including the NAACP magazine *The Crisis*, Langston Hughes and Richard Nugent's *Fire!!*, and the National Urban League's *Opportunity: A Journal of Negro Life*, which chronicled cultural advancements during the Harlem Renaissance. Bennett also published in *The Crisis*, as well as in volumes including William Stanley Braithwaite's *Anthology of Magazine Verse* (1927), *Yearbook of American Poetry* (1927), Countee Cullen's *Caroling Dusk* (1927), and James Weldon Johnson's *The Book of American Negro Poetry* (1931).

She is perhaps best known for her short story "Wedding Day," which appeared in the magazine *Fire!!* The story explores the dynamics of interracial relationships based on gender, race, and class. Another of her contributions to the Harlem Renaissance was her acclaimed short novel *Poets Evening*. It contributed to self-awareness in Black communities, resulting in many African Americans coming to terms with their identities and accepting themselves.

Her influential poem "Fantasy" put emphasis on the racial pride of African Americans as well as on the possibilities available for women. *The Ebony Flute*, a literary column inspired by William Rose Bennet's poem "Harlem," was another way Bennett contributed to the Harlem Renaissance by distributing news about the many creative thinkers of that movement.

Bennett married educator and writer Richard Crosscup, who was of European descent, in 1940. It was not considered a socially acceptable relationship at the time. On suspicion that Bennett was a communist, the FBI investigated her constantly in 1941. Although no conclusive or evidentiary findings were made, they continued to reinvestigate her periodically until 1959. This experience caused her to withdraw from the public eye, and she began working as a secretary for the Consumers Union. The couple moved to Kutztown, Pennsylvania, where they opened Buttonwood Hollow Antiques, an antique shop.

NNEDI OKORAFOR:
Courageous Weaver of Cultures

Nnedi Okorafor is an internationally known award-winning author of science fiction, fantasy, and works of magic realism incorporating African culture, characterization, and settings. She was born in 1974, the daughter of Nigerian Igbo parents who came to the United States to further their educations and were stranded in America when the Nigerian Civil War broke out. Her father was a heart surgeon. From an early age, young Nnedi often visited Nigeria. She went on to become a nationally known track and tennis star for Homewood-Flossmoor High School in Illinois, as well as achieving academic success in science and mathematics; she planned to pursue a career in entomology. But when she was nineteen, a preexisting scoliosis condition worsened, and though surgeons tried to straighten and fuse her spine, she experienced a rare complication following the operation and ended up paralyzed from the waist down.

It was at this point that she began for the first time to write little stories—'little' in a literal sense, as she inscribed them in the margins of one of her science fiction books. With intensive physical therapy the following summer, she was able to literally get back on her feet, but her career as an athlete was finished, as she then needed a cane even to walk. A close friend suggested that she take a creative writing course; by the end of the semester, she had begun to write her first novel. She went on to earn a number of writing-related degrees: a master's in journalism from Michigan State, and both a master's and PhD in literature and creative writing from the University of Illinois at Chicago. She also graduated from the Clarion Writers Workshop in Lansing, Michigan, in 2001. During her sophomore undergraduate year, she wrote her first serious story, which she set in Nigeria. She wanted to set stories in Africa because so few stories used it as a setting, and she wanted people of color and girls to play important parts in her narratives, since previously most important characters in speculative fiction had been white and male. She also cites Nigeria itself as her "muse," since she has been deeply influenced by Nigerian folklore, mythology, and mysticism. She also married and had a daughter (Anyaugo, or Anya) during these years of academic study.

In 2001, she received the Hurston-Wright award for her story "Amphibious Green;" since then, many of her short stories have been published in myriad anthologies and magazines, as well as in her own short story collection, *Kabu Kabu* (2013), which includes a foreword written by Whoopi Goldberg. Following her first short story award, she went on to write two prizewinning young adult books, *Zahrah the Windseeker* (2005) and *The Shadow Speaker* (2007), as well as a children's book, *Long Juju Man* (2009). When she tackled writing a novel for adults after the passing of her father with *Who Fears Death* (2010), the book won the 2011 World Fantasy Award for Best Novel as well as other accolades; it is currently in development as an HBO drama series with George R.R. Martin of *Game of Thrones* fame on board as executive producer. Her reputation continued to grow with the Akata series for young adults, followed by two novels for adults: *Lagoon* (2014) and *The Book of Phoenix* (2015), a prequel to *Who Fears Death* that *The New York Times* called a "triumph." That same publication once profiled Okorafor's work under the title, "Weapons of Mass Creation."

Okorafor is perhaps best known for her Binti trilogy; it began with the novella *Binti* (2015), which won both the Nebula and Hugo Awards for best novella in 2016. Sequels *Binti: Home* (2017) and *Binti: The Night Masquerade* (2018) were both finalist nominees for the Hugo Award in the same category. Concurrent with these releases, a Nigerian film company optioned a hybrid short story of hers involving both witchcraft and science for adaptation as a short film titled *Hello, Rain*, which premiered at the International Short Film Festival Oberhausen in 2018. She has also written a number of comic books for Marvel based on *Black Panther*, including 2018's *Wakanda Forever* and *Shuri*, focusing on the title character, a princess of the fictional land of Wakanda. *New York Times* writer Alexandra Alter said of Okorafor that her work frequently examines "weighty social issues: racial and gender inequality, political violence, the destruction of the environment, genocide, and corruption" using "the framework of fantasy." Nnedi Okorafor is an associate professor at SUNY in Buffalo, New York, and splits her time between Buffalo and Illinois.

NISI SHAWL:
Teaching Diversity
through Her Artistry

Nisi Shawl is an African American journalist and editor who is best known as the author of several dozen science fiction and fantasy short stories. Both in her own writing and as a creative writing teacher, she communicates how speculative fiction can better mirror real-world diversity of not only gender, race, age, and sexual orientation, but also differing levels of physical ability and other socioeconomic variables. With Cynthia Ward, she coauthored the creative writing handbook *Writing the Other: Bridging Cultural Differences for Successful Fiction*, a follow-up to the workshops of the same name, which Shawl has taught for the last decade. *Strange Horizons* reviewer Genevieve Williams said of the handbook, "Much of what Shawl and Ward advocate is, quite simply, good practice: the avoidance of clichés, flat characters, unintended effects, and other hallmarks of lazy writing."

Born in Kalamazoo, Michigan, in 1955, as a small child, young Nisi told fantastical stories of her own invention to her sister. Precociously intelligent, she started college at the University of Michigan College of Literature, Science, and the Arts in Ann Arbor at only sixteen, but feeling alienated, she dropped out two weeks before finals. She moved into Cosmic Plateau, an affordable shared household where her rent was only sixty-five dollars per month, and worked part-time at all sorts of jobs while honing her craft as a writer; she even played in a band for a time as well as doing spoken word performances of her written works at cafes, parks, and museums.

Her first professional short story sale came in 1989; "I Was a Teenage Genetic Engineer" was published in the literary journal *Semiotext(e)*, alongside works by such authors as William S. Burroughs, William Gibson, J.G. Ballard, and Bruce Sterling. In 1992, in a fateful twist, Shawl went to a cyberpunk symposium in Detroit; because of her story having been published in *Semiotext(e)*, a publication which pioneering cyberpunk author Bruce Sterling thought none of the attendees would have even encountered, she made networking connections there with cyberpunk authors Sterling, Pat Cadigan, and John Shirley. Shirley offered to read Shawl's short fiction; he thought that she possessed talent as a writer and advised her to participate in the Clarion West Writers' Workshop, where he and Cadigan were teaching that year. Nisi Shawl later said of the experience, "At

Clarion West, I learned in six weeks what six years at the University could never have taught me." Discussions with other workshop participants eventually led her to create a *Writing the Other* essay and class, from which she and Cynthia Ward, whom she met at Clarion West, cocreated the handbook. This, along with positive experiences at another writing program in the Puget Sound area, Cottages at Hedgebrook on Whidbey Island, provided the impetus for Shawl to relocate to Seattle following a divorce. She is now a member of Clarion West's board of directors. She has written dozens of reviews for the *Seattle Times* and *Ms.* magazine and has lectured at Stanford and Duke universities.

Her short story collection *Filter House* was chosen by *Publishers Weekly* as one of their best books of 2008, and won the James Tiptree Jr. Award for science fiction and fantasy "which expands or explores our understanding of gender," sharing the latter prize for 2008 with Patrick Ness. Shawl has also edited a number of speculative fiction collections; her work as an anthologist has encompassed feminist, Afrofuturist, and LGBTQ+ speculative fiction, including twice coediting homages to lesbian and gay novelists of color: *Strange Matings: Science Fiction, Feminism, African American Voices, and Octavia E. Butler* and *Stories for Chip: A Tribute to Samuel R. Delany*, both published in 2015. Shawl herself has stated that she identifies as bisexual. Since then, she has coedited the 2018 collection *Exploring Dark Short Fiction 3* as well as editing *People of Color Take Over Fantastic Stories of the Imagination* (2017) and *New Suns* (2019).

Her 2016 novel *Everfair* broke new ground as well; rather than waxing nostalgic about the colonialist aspects of the Victorian era as many steampunk novels do, it took these issues on, creating an alternate history in which the British Fabian Society decides to create an African sanctuary for those fleeing the tyranny of Belgian King Leopold II, who in the actual nineteenth century brutally enslaved the indigenous people of the Congo in order to profit from the local resource of natural rubber. The new and eponymously named nation of Everfair, like the fictional country of Wakanda, works to develop the technology to protect themselves from rapacious European interests; the novel went on to be nominated for both Hugo and Campbell awards.

OCTAVIA E. BUTLER:
Dreaming How Humanity Can Transcend Hierarchy

Octavia E. Butler was a Black American science fiction author known for her novels, which explored futuristic utopian/dystopian themes. Young Octavia was the only child of Octavia Guy Butler, a housemaid, and Laurice Butler, a shoeshine man who died when she was seven. She was raised in a strict Baptist household by her grandmother and her mother, whom she often accompanied to her housecleaning work sites, where they were expected to use only the back door to enter the house. She was extremely shy and turned to books for stimulation; after starting with fairy tales and horse stories, she was drawn to science fiction magazines featuring the work of writers including Zenna Henderson, Theodore Sturgeon, and John Brunner. At ten, she pleaded with her mother to buy her a manual Remington typewriter, at which she composed stories for countless hours using two-finger typing; at twelve, she drafted the beginnings of what would later become her Patternist series of science fiction novels. At age thirteen, when her aunt told her that Negroes couldn't be writers, though perhaps temporarily daunted, she persevered. While working days and attending night school as a freshman at Pasadena City College, she earned her first money as a writer by winning a college-wide short story contest in 1968.

Butler continued her education at California State University Los Angeles and then at UCLA, where one of her writing instructors was the noted science fiction author Harlan Ellison. Encouraged by Ellison, in 1970, she began her writing career in earnest. In 1976, she published *Patternmaster*, the first of her five-volume Patternist series about an elite group of telepaths governed by Doro, a four-thousand-year-old immortal African man who had to periodically move his consciousness to new bodies to survive. *Patternmaster* was followed by *Mind of My Mind* (1977), *Survivor* (1978), *Wild Seed* (1980), and *Clay's Ark* (1984). While in the midst of producing the Patternist series, Butler released the novel *Kindred* in 1979; it tells the story of a modern Black woman sent back in time to an antebellum plantation, where she poses as a slave in order to carry out the rescue of her own ancestor, a white slave owner. *Kindred* was later adapted as a graphic novel released in 2017.

Later novels included the Xenogenesis trilogy: *Dawn: Xenogenesis* (1987), *Adulthood Rites* (1988), and *Imago* (1989). That trilogy was followed by *The Parable of the Sower* (1993), *The Parable of the Talents* (1998), and *Fledgling* (2005). Butler began to achieve serious recognition when her short story "Speech Sounds" won a Hugo Award in 1984; a year later, her story *Bloodchild*, which told the story of human male slaves who incubated the eggs of their alien masters, won both the Hugo and Nebula awards. In 1995, she became the first science fiction writer ever to be awarded a MacArthur Foundation Fellowship, and she received a PEN Award for lifetime achievement in 2000. Her last book was the science fiction/vampire novel *Fledgling*, the tale of a West Coast vampire community in a state of symbiosis with humans, seen through the eyes of a young female hybrid vampire. Butler's work is associated with the Afrofuturism genre, defined as "speculative fiction that treats African American themes and addresses African American concerns in the context of twentieth century technoculture."

> "Simple peck-order bullying is only the beginning of the kind of hierarchical behavior that can lead to racism, sexism, ethnocentrism, classism, and all the other 'isms' that cause so much suffering in the world."
>
> **—Octavia E. Butler,**
>
> American science fiction author; she went on to write many stories despite being told by an aunt that Black people can't be writers

EDWIDGE DANTICAT:
Immigrant Author, Mother, Daughter, Lover

Edwidge Danticat is a Haitian American short story writer and novelist; born in 1969, she started writing while in Haiti before coming to the US at age twelve to live in a Haitian neighborhood in Brooklyn, New York. As a disoriented teenage immigrant, she found solace in literature. At Barnard College in New York City, she originally intended to study nursing, but ended up graduating with a BA in French literature before going on to earn a master's degree in creative writing from Brown University in 1993. Her master's thesis formed the basis for her novel *Breath, Eyes, Memory* (1994), which became an Oprah's Book Club selection in 1998.

Her novels since include *Krik? Krak!*, *The Farming of Bones*, *The Dew Breaker*, *Create Dangerously*, and *Claire of the Sea Light*, as well as her youth fiction works *Anacaona*, *Behind the Mountains*, *Eight Days*, *The Last Mapou*, *Mama's Nightingale*, and *Untwine*. Her memoir *Brother, I'm Dying* won the National Book Critics Circle Award for autobiography in 2008. She has edited several collections of essays and authored a travel narrative, *After the Dance: A Walk Through Carnival in Jacmel, Haiti*, which gives readers an inside look at the cultural legacy of the land of her birth. Danticat is best known for her exploration of the developing identity of Haitian immigrants, the politics of the diaspora, especially as related to the experience of women, and mother/daughter relationships. Since the publication of her first novel in 1994, she has consistently won accolades for her literary accomplishments.

ZADIE SMITH:
Transforming Assumptions
with Her Writing

Born Sadie Smith in 1975 to a Jamaican mother and an English father, at age fourteen, she changed her name to **Zadie**. An early interest in jazz singing gave way to the pursuit of a career in writing. While studying English literature at King's College, her short stories attracted the attention of a publisher, and her professional career was assured before she even graduated. Her first novel, *White Teeth* (2000), became an immediate bestseller. Since then, she has been a prolific writer of novels, short fiction, and essays. Her novels include *The Autograph Man* (2002), *On Beauty* (2005), *NW* (2012), *Swing Time* (2016), *The Fraud* (2019), and *The Wife of Willesden* (2021); and in 2019, she also published a short fiction collection, *Grand Union: Stories*.

In 2002, Smith was elected a fellow of the Royal Society of Literature. Among her many accolades, her debut novel *White Teeth* received the James Tait Black Memorial Prize, the Whitbread First Novel Award, and the Guardian First Book Award; her second book, *On Beauty*, won the Orange Prize for Fiction. In 2017, she was awarded the Langston Hughes Medal by the City College of New York. Since 2010, Zadie Smith has been a tenured professor in the creative writing department at New York University.

ANGIE THOMAS:
"Be Roses That Grow in the Concrete"

Angie Thomas was born, raised, and still lives in Jackson, Mississippi, as her accent reveals. She was a rapper as a teenager; her greatest accomplishment was an article about her music with a picture of her in *Right On!* magazine. Besides her skills and experience with hip-hop, she holds a BFA in creative writing from Belhaven University. In 2015, she was the inaugural winner of the Walter Dean Myers Grant, awarded by the children's nonprofit We Need Diverse

Books. Her award-winning debut novel, *The Hate U Give*, was on the *New York Times* bestseller list for nearly two years; it was released as a major motion picture in 2018 and was warmly received by both critics and audiences. Her second book, a young adult novel titled *On the Come Up* (2019), tells the story of an aspiring teenage rapper who causes controversy on her road to making it big. As of this writing, it is being adapted for cinematic release after positive reviews from *The New York Times* and *The Washington Post*.

JE/MYN WARD:
"I Burn, and I Hope"

Although **Jesmyn Ward** was born in 1977 in Berkeley, California, she was raised in DeLisle, Mississippi. She received a BA in 1999, followed in 2000 by an MA in media studies, both from Stanford University. Soon after she received an MFA in creative writing in 2005 from the University of Michigan, she and her family had their home in DeLisle severely damaged by Hurricane Katrina. While working at the University of New Orleans, Ward had to commute daily through neighborhoods that had been destroyed by the hurricane. Continually reminded of the tragedy, she was unable to write creatively for three years; in 2008, just when she was about to give up on writing and enroll in a nursing program, her first novel, *Where the Line Bleeds*, was accepted for publication. It was quickly recognized as significant, and in 2009, it received a Black Caucus of the American Library Association (BCALA) Honor Award. Both her fiction and nonfiction are largely centered around the experience and struggles of Black individuals living in the rural Gulf Coast.

Her two later novels, *Salvage the Bones* (2011) and *Sing, Unburied, Sing* (2017), both won National Book awards for fiction. Between the publication of these two fiction works, her 2013 memoir *Men We Reaped* won the Chicago Tribune Heartland Prize and the Media for a Just Society Award. Other recognition followed, including a MacArthur Genius Grant, a Stegner Fellowship, a John and Renee Grisham Writers Residency, and the Strauss Living Prize, among other accolades. Ward also edited *The Fire This Time: A New Generation Speaks About Race* (2016), a modern analysis that carries into the present the concerns and observations of James Baldwin's classic 1993 examination of racism in America. Ward is currently an associate professor of creative writing at Tulane University and lives in Mississippi.

ALICE WALKER:
The Color of Passion

Though she currently lives in California, Pulitzer Prize-winning author **Alice Walker** has never forgotten her rural Georgian roots. "You look at old photographs of Southern Blacks and you see it—a real determination and proof of a moral center that is absolutely bedrock to the land," she once said. Certainly that strength is brilliantly displayed in her most famous novel, *The Color Purple*, particularly in its portrayals of Southern Black women. *The Color Purple* draws on her memories of the landscape and language of the South.

Walker was born in 1944, the eighth child of poor sharecroppers in Eatonton, Georgia. Her mother encouraged her writing, going so far as to buy young Alice a typewriter even though she herself made less than twenty dollars a week. In 1967, after college, Walker married a white man, and the duo lived in Mississippi as the first legally married interracial couple in the state. Her marriage, she claims, had a negative effect on her career because it angered Black reviewers, who ignored her earlier works, including *In Love and Trouble* and *Meridian*.

It was her third novel, *The Color Purple*, that rocketed her to fame in 1983 (winning both the Pulitzer Prize and the National Book Award) and embroiled her in controversy, particularly with the male members of the African American community, who claimed the work reinforced negative stereotypes about Black men. The subsequent movie by Steven Spielberg in 1985 only fanned the flames of the imbroglio. However, women of all races strongly embraced the novel and identified with Celie, a fourteen-year-old girl who is repeatedly raped by the man she believes to be her father. The children of this union are adopted by a missionary family in Africa. The novel takes the form of letters between Celie and her sister Nettie, who works for the family that has adopted Celie's children.

The literary heir of Zora Neale Hurston and Flannery O'Connor, the prolific "womanist," as she calls herself, has penned novels, short stories, poetry, and essays—seventeen volumes in all so far. Each reveals her deep commitment to social justice, feminism, and particularly, African American women, as seen through her unique inner vision, a vision she has said she began to develop after she became blind in one eye when one of her brothers accidentally shot her with a BB gun. The loss of sight in one eye forced her inward, and she began to carefully observe the people around her. By writing, she has noted, "I'm really paying homage to the people I love, the people who are thought to be dumb and backward but who taught me to see beauty."

She believes strongly in the power of art to help change the world and the artist's responsibility to that power—ideas she expressed in her collection of essays, *In Search of Our Mothers' Gardens*. In an audiotape entitled *My Life as Myself*, she spoke of her activism: "My way of fighting back is to understand [injustice] and then to create a work that expresses what I understand."

———

Black literature has a long, complicated history. The themes of Black writing are as varied as Black people themselves, but many Black women writers have focused on racism, slavery, and social equality. Today, Black literature is part of mainstream America. Many Black female writers create bestsellers and win awards, and their work is studied at colleges and universities. This was not always the case. The earliest Black women writers often had to go to England or other countries to publish their work. In many cases, writers weren't discovered until long after their deaths. The oldest known piece of Black literature in America was a poem written by **Lucy Terry** titled "Bars Fight." It was written in 1746 in response to an Indian attack in Deerfield, Massachusetts, but it was not published until 1854, long after Phillis Wheatley's collections of poetry were published. **Phillis Wheatley** was the first known Black female poet to publish her work in the New World. She famously met with George Washington at his encampment. Phyllis was enslaved but was awarded her freedom. Her owners had taught her to read and write when she was a young girl, and she was fluent in several languages, including Greek. The first novel by a Black American writer published in America was **Harriet Wilson**'s *Our Nig*; published in 1859, the novel depicts the difficulties of life for Northern Black people.

The middle of the nineteenth century saw an increase in the number of Black female Americans publishing their writing thanks to the genre of the slave narrative. A slave narrative usually tells the story of a slave's escape to freedom. It is estimated that more than 6,000 slaves from the United States and the Caribbean wrote their account of slavery down, and roughly 150 of these were published as books or pamphlets. The reasons for writing a slave narrative are very clear. The former slaves wanted people to see their humanity and wanted better living conditions for those still enslaved. The slave narratives were popular among abolitionists, who used them as evidence of slavery's evils in their fight to end the practice of enslavement. Among the most famous slave narratives is **Harriet Jacobs**'s *Incidents in the Life of a Slave Girl*, a story that tells the author's struggle to find freedom and of her fight to win freedom for her two children.

After the Civil War, Black female writers found more opportunity to publish their writing. For the first time in American history, it was legal for Black people in the South to read and write. Black newspapers began to publish articles and offered a place for Black women authors to submit their nonfiction and creative writing. Journalists such as **Jennie Carter** began to build large followings of readers. **Mary Weston Fordham** published a book of poetry called *Magnolia Leaves* in 1897, and **Frances E. Harper** wrote four novels, several collections of poetry, and many further poems, short stories, essays, and letters.

As a result of the Great Migration out of the South and away from Jim Crow laws, Black literature blossomed in the 1920s to 1940s during the Harlem Renaissance. Langston Hughes began publishing his poetry during this era, along with **Zora Neale Hurston**, whose novel, *Their Eyes Were Watching God*, has become a classic example of Black literature. The Harlem Renaissance also produced **Jean Toomer**, whose book *Cane* is a collection of short stories, poems, and sketches about rural and city life. **Dorothy West**'s novel *The Living is Easy* explored the lives of upper-class Black families. The Harlem Renaissance was notable because for the first time, Black authors were being read by a mainstream American audience.

During the Civil Rights Era, Black authors continued to write and publish. Black female poets such as **Gwendolyn Brooks**, the first Black American to win the Pulitzer Prize, **Nikki Giovanni**, and **Sonia Sanchez** became popular during the Civil Rights Era.

A number of Black playwrights began producing their plays on stage, including **Lorraine Hansberry**, whose play *A Raisin in the Sun* won the New York Drama Critics' Circle Award in 1959.

Starting in the 1970s, the Black Arts Movement saw the works of Black authors take over the mainstream and begin to receive recognition for the quality of writing by hitting the bestseller lists and winning awards. **Toni Morrison** helped define the Black Arts Movement with her novels and editing work. **Alice Walker** won both the American Book Award and the Pulitzer Prize for her novel *The Color Purple*. Steven Spielberg later made *The Color Purple* into a film, and a stage version of the novel has been performed in theaters.

American publishing still has a long way to go in terms of publishing Black female writers as much as they publish white writers, but there are many more Black writers publishing and winning awards today than ever before. In 2003, **ZZ Packer** published her debut collection of short stories *Drinking Coffee Elsewhere*. ZZ has won a number of awards, including the Rona Jaffee Foundation Writers' Award, the Whiting Award, a PEN/Faulkner Award, and an Alex Award. Cameroonian American writer **Imbolo Mbue** wrote her debut novel *Behold the Dreamers* while she was out of work during an economic recession. In 2014, she signed a million-dollar contract to publish the book, which went on to win the PEN/Faulkner Award for fiction and the Blue Metropolis Words to Change Award. Best known for her book *Miracle's Boys*, **Jacqueline Woodson** has won the Newbery Award and was granted a MacArthur Foundation genius grant.

Indefatigable

The list of Black female writers to date is a substantial roster, and they come from many different countries around the globe. **Mitta Xinindlu** knows ten languages and is 100 percent fluent in three! Guadeloupean novelist, critic, and playwright **Maryse Conde´** has written mind-blowing novels that have been translated into over seven different languages. Though born in South Africa, **Bessie Head** is usually considered Botswana's most influential writer; after leaving a loveless marriage, she took a job as a

teacher, but she had to bite the headmaster after several unwanted sexual advances. Born in St. John's, Antigua, **Jamaica Kincaid** worked as an au pair to support herself after moving to the United States in 1966 at age seventeen. Later, she was able to gain a college education; now, her work is popular in college classrooms. Her short story "Girl" is often assigned as part of literature curricula. Born in Jamaica in 1960, **Nalo Hopkinson** is a Canadian speculative fiction author and editor who has also been a professor of creative writing at UC Riverside since 2011; her teaching focuses on the fantasy, science fiction, and magic realism genres, and she is a member of a faculty research cluster in science fiction. Her writing draws on myth and folklore as well as Caribbean language, history, and storytelling traditions. Nigerian writer **Chimamanda Ngozi Adichie** began writing at the age of seven. She is a well-known feminist who found power in sharing Black stories— which were her own stories as well. Black women writers are indefatigable. Born to a family of Haitian descent, **Roxane Gay** is an American professor, author, editor, and commentator. She began writing essays as a teenager; her writing was sparked by having survived a sexual assault at age twelve. Her fiction and nonfiction explore a variety of issues and challenges relating to race, gender, sexual identity, privilege, body image, and the immigrant experience. **Margaret Walker** took thirty years to write her novel *Jubilee*; critics raved about how the book brought life to the characters.

DAISY BATES:
Fighting the System and Winning!

Daisy Bates was one of the first civil rights warriors called into action in the fight for desegregation. Together with her husband, L.C. Bates, a Black man who had been educated as a journalist, she took over a Little Rock newspaper, the *Arkansas State Press*, and turned it into a platform for "the people," reporting crimes committed against Black people that the white paper ignored. Bates worked as a reporter, covering with complete honesty, for example, the cold-blooded murder of a Black soldier by military police. The white business community was outraged over the *State Press*'s coverage: They feared the army would leave their town and withdraw all advertising. However, the bravery of Daisy and L.C. Bates in the face of brutality to Black people curtailed these crimes, and Little Rock became a more liberated town despite itself.

Then the movement toward desegregation heated up, with Daisy Bates again right in the thick of things. The Supreme Court had declared segregation of schools unconstitutional in May of 1954, giving Southern schools the chance to describe how and when they would make the required changes. The local school board had responded by saying that they would take on the notion of integration "gradually." Little Rock's Black community was up in arms about the foot-dragging, and after butting heads with school officials in many stony-faced meetings, they opted to take matters into their own hands. The state and local NAACP decided that they would try to enroll the students in the segregated schools and build cases of denied admission in order to bring a legal challenge to the policy of gradualism. As president of the NAACP in Little Rock, Bates worked with the *State Press* and other papers to publicize this flouting of the Supreme Court's ruling. Finally, in 1957, they decided to integrate the high school, come hell or high water. The children who put their bodies on the line became famous overnight as "Daisy's children" and suffered personal agony for the cause of racial injustice.

When nine children were selected to attend "whites only" Central High School, Bates acted as their escort and protector. Answering a poll by school officials, the group of young heroes and sheroes consisted of: Carlotta Walls, Thelma Mothershed, Melba Patillo, Ernest Green, Terrence Roberts, Gloria Ray, Minnijean Brown, Jefferson Thomas, and Elizabeth Eckford. When Little Rock school superintendent Virgil Blossom decreed that no adults could accompany the Black students, Bates called all of their homes and told them there would be a change of plans.

Elizabeth Eckford's family had no telephone, so she showed up on opening day–to be faced by an angry white mob who also attacked reporters and photographers. The mob siege lasted seventeen days until a thousand paratroopers showed up in response to orders from the White House to carry out enforcing the order of legal integration of the school.

However, the students were on their own once inside, prey to taunts, shoving, and threats of violence. Daisy Bates continued to protect and advise the children throughout the ordeal, accompanying them to every meeting with a school official when racial incidents happened. The struggle at Little Rock was only the first in a round of actions that ultimately led to full legal desegregation. Though difficult, the victory was entirely to Bates and her "children," who showed the nation that you could stand up to hatred and ignorance with honesty and dignity. You can fight a losing battle and win.

> **"No man or woman who tries to pursue an ideal in his or her own way is without enemies."**
>
> **—Daisy Bates,**
> civil rights activist and newspaper publisher
> who documented the battle to end segregation
> in Arkansas

IDA B. WELLS:
Journalist for Justice

Ida Bell Wells-Barnett was an African American journalist and advocate of women's rights, including the right to vote. Though she was born a slave in 1862 in Holly Springs, Mississippi, only six months later the Emancipation Proclamation freed all slaves. Even though they were legally free citizens, her family faced racial prejudice and discrimination while living in Mississippi. Her father helped start Shaw University, and Ida received schooling there, but when she was sixteen, her parents and one of her siblings died of yellow fever. This meant that as the eldest, Ida had to stop going to school and start taking care of her eight sisters and brothers. Since the family desperately needed money, Ida ingeniously convinced a county school official that she was eighteen and managed to obtain a job as a teacher. In 1882, she moved to her aunt's in Nashville, living there with several siblings, and at last was able to continue her education at Fisk University.

A direct experience of prejudice in 1884 electrifyingly catalyzed Wells's sense of the need to advocate for justice. While traveling from Memphis to Nashville, she bought a first-class train ticket, but was outraged when the crew told her to move to the car for African Americans. Refusing, Wells was forced off the train bodily; rather than giving in and giving up, she sued the railroad in circuit court and gained a judgment forcing them to pay her $500. Sadly, the state Supreme Court later overturned the decision; but this experience motivated her to write about Southern racial politics and prejudice. Various Black publications published her articles, written under the nom-de-plume "Iola." Wells later became an owner of two papers, the *Memphis Free Speech and Headlight* and *Free Speech*.

Besides her journalistic and publishing work, she also worked as a teacher at one of Memphis's Black-only public schools. She became a vocal critic of the condition of these segregated schools. This advocacy caused her to be fired from her job in 1891. The next year, three African Americans who were partners in owning a store clashed with the white owner of a store nearby who felt they were competing too successfully for local business; when the white store owner showed up with several allies and attacked their store, the Black store owners ended up shooting several white men while defending their business. The three Black men were taken to jail, but never had their day in court—a lynch mob dragged them out and murdered all three men. Moved to action by this horrible tragedy, Wells started writing about the lynchings of a friend and others and went on to do in-depth investigative reporting of lynching in America, risking her life to do so.

While away in New York, Wells was told that her office had been trashed by a mob, and that if she ever came back to Memphis, she would be killed. She remained in the North and published an in-depth article on lynching for the *New York Age*, a paper owned by a former slave; she then toured abroad, lecturing on the issue in the hope of enlisting the support of pro-reform whites. When she found out that Black exhibitors were banned at the 1893 World's Columbian Exposition, she published a pamphlet with the support and backing of famed freed slave and abolitionist Frederick Douglass, as well as "A Red Record," a personal report on lynchings in America.

In 1896, Wells founded the National Association of Colored Women; and in 1898, she took her anti-lynching campaign to the White House and led a protest in Washington, DC, to urge President McKinley to act. She was a founding member of the NAACP, but later cut ties with the organization, feeling that it wasn't sufficiently focused on taking action. Wells also worked on behalf of all women and was a part of the National Equal Rights League; she continuously fought for women's suffrage. She even ran for the state senate in 1930, but her health failed the next year, and she died of kidney disease at the age of sixty-eight. Well's life is a testament to courage in the face of danger.

> **"I felt that one had better die fighting against injustice than to die like a dog or rat in a trap. I had already determined to sell my life as dearly as possible if attacked. I felt if I could take one lyncher with me, this would even up the score a little bit."**
>
> **—Ida B. Wells,**
> journalist and activist who led an anti-lynching crusade in the United States in the 1890s

Whether they are fiction writers or poets, these writers have expanded the notion of what constitutes "story," and have made the "other" the mainstream. Black women writers sell big when their stories are given a platform and their voices are heard. In creating worlds from their visions, they ignite the creative spark for future generations.

chapter three

RHYTHM & RHYME

POETS & LITERARY PIONEERS

L ike their counterparts in fiction, Black women poets
are all about breathing new life into our language.
Drawing on the syncopated rhythms of jazz, the gut-
wrenching cadences of the blues, and the long-held
tradition of call-and-response songs and chants, Black
female poets create worlds with their words. Poets such as
Claudia Rankine and **M.J. Fievre** bend genre in their work,

combining the theatrical with the poetic, bursting forth with shockingly raw and new genres. Wordsmiths like **Audre Lorde** and **Warsan Shire** are reinvigorating the canon and bringing new means of expression to the table.

Black women have been expressing themselves in poetry since before they left Africa. They have been making themselves heard in America since colonial times; what would become the United States was still a fledgling colony when the first Black poet picked up her quill and began to write. **Lucy Terry** is thought to have first sung her breakthrough poem "The Bars Fight" way back in the 1700s. George Sheldon, a Deerfield historian, declared Lucy's ballad to be "the first rhymed narration of an American slave." Born circa 1753, **Phillis Wheatley** became the first published Black American woman poet in the American colonies. Captured in the region of Senegal and Gambia at about the age of seven, Wheatley was raised in slavery by a progressive white family who taught her to read and write and encouraged her to develop her talents. White publishers, however, were so skeptical that an African slave could write poetry that they forced her to undergo an examination to determine if she could author her own poems. She passed the exam and her book was published.

Nearly two hundred years later, Wheatley's legacy entered a new era when **Rita Dove** became the first Black Poet Laureate of the United States. Black women poets are taking the national stage with their poetry: **Amanda Gorman** and **Maya Angelou** have each brought their poetry to the inaugurations of President Joe Biden and President Bill Clinton (respectively). The achievements of Black female poets in America bely the notion that Black women should sit still and be quiet. These women are loud and proud, and not afraid to face the nation.

MAYA ANGELOU:
How the Caged Bird Sings

Marguerite Johnson's childhood was marked by the hardship of the Depression years in which she grew up. Her parents divorced and packed her off to live with her granny, "Momma" Henderson, who eked out a living running a little general store in Stamps, Arkansas. Marguerite, known as Maya, attended church devotedly with Momma, who gave her stability and taught her the importance of values and a strong work ethic. The young girl found love and roots with her grandmother and the congregation at their church.

But tragedy struck when she visited her mother in St. Louis for eight months. Her mother had a boyfriend who spent a lot of time at her mother's house and often touched and hugged the seven-year-old in an excessively familiar way, but in her innocence, she mistook it for a father's love. Later, he raped her, and Angelou felt guilty and responsible for his jailing and subsequent death at the hands of other inmates who exacted their own brand of justice on a child molester. She became catatonic from the trauma of this onslaught of catastrophic violence in her world. With the support of her family and an adult friend, Bertha Flowers, who introduced her to literature, she gradually reentered the world, eventually speaking after five years and graduating first in her eighth-grade class.

Angelou and her mother then moved to San Francisco, where her mother ran a boardinghouse and worked as a professional gambler. She met many colorful characters among the boarders and threw herself into school, where she flourished. Young Maya got pregnant at sixteen and took on the full responsibilities of motherhood with the birth of her son, Guy. For a few years, Angelou walked on the wild side: working at a Creole restaurant, waitressing at a bar in San Diego, and even an accidental and brief stint as a madam for two lesbian prostitutes. After a two-year marriage to a white man, she started dancing at the Purple Onion and got into show biz when she joined the road show for *Porgy and Bess*, which toured Africa and Europe. After cowriting "Cabaret for Freedom" with Godfrey Cambridge for the Southern Christian Leadership Conference, Angelou drew Martin Luther King Jr.'s attention for her talents and her contribution to the Civil Rights Movement, and he invited her to serve as an SCLC coordinator.

Maya Angelou's career was absolutely astonishing after this point: She lived in Egypt with Guy and her lover, a South African freedom fighter, and worked in Ghana writing for *The African Review*. She remained involved with the theater, writing and performing in plays, acting in *Roots*, and writing several volumes of poetry, as well as the script and music for the televised movie adaptation of her autobiography. But it is for the six bestselling volumes of her autobiography, starting with *I Know Why the Caged Bird Sings*, that she will go down in literary history; *The New York*

Times called her "one of the geniuses of Afro-American serial autobiography." Written with captivating honesty, color, and verve, they are read by youth and adults alike for their inspirational message. Listen to this powerful passage from *I Know Why the Caged Bird Sings*: "If growing up is painful for the Southern Black girl, being aware of her displacement is the rust on the razor that threatens the throat. It is an unnecessary insult." When she was criticized for not being completely factual as a writer, she responded, "There's a world of difference between truth and facts. Facts can obscure truth."

Maya Angelou, a name combined from a nickname her brother called her and a variation on her first husband's name, truly reinvented herself. No moment in her wonderfully colorful life illustrates this as much as her reading of her beautiful poem, "On the Pulse of Morning," at President Bill Clinton's first inauguration. She had come a long way from a scared and silent little seven-year-old to a woman come fully into her power and unafraid to share it with the world.

> **"The ability to control one's own destiny...comes from constant hard work and courage."**
>
> **—Maya Angelou,**
>
> American poet, memoirist, and civil rights activist; a sexual assault left her mute when she was young, until a teacher helped her to read and speak again

BELL HOOKS:
An Untamed Tongue

Born Gloria Jean Watkins in the small town of Hopkinville, Kentucky, in 1952, poet, feminist theorist, and professor **bell hooks** grew up as one of six kids who saw their father working as a janitor and their mother cleaning houses for white people. bell was in the first round of desegregated classes and grieved for the loss of community and safety that desegregation caused: "It hurt to leave behind memories, schools that were 'ours,' places that honored us." She was raised to be polite and mind her manners, but she "had a mouth." For talking back and saying what she really thought, she was chided by a neighbor as being "akin to Bell Hooks [her maternal grandmother—a sharp-tongued woman]...." Gloria was expected to be a sweet Southern girl, quiet, obedient, and pleasing. She was not to display the wild streak that characterized women on her mother's side. With that, she changed her name and continued to find her own voice and speak out.

She found her calling at a young age—by the time she was ten, she was composing poems. Later, while working as a telephone operator to pay for classes at Stanford, nineteen-year-old hooks shared her writing with her coworkers, working-class Black women who nurtured her talent and encouraged her to tell the world about being Black and a woman. While she continued to write poetry in later years, her fame as a writer has come from critical essays on race, gender, and class.

After earning a PhD in English literature, she taught English and African American studies at various institutions around the country, including Yale, Oberlin, San Francisco State, and City College of New York. Her work was first published in 1981 in the book *Ain't I A Woman*, a title quoting and honoring the great shero Sojourner Truth. Her book had an immediate impact and was named one of the top twenty most important women's books. More importantly to hooks, she received hundreds of letters from Black women, including many poor and working-class readers all over America who told them *Ain't I A Woman* had changed their lives. For hooks, the goal of a fully inclusive feminism rather than an "old girl's school" of Ivy League white women was on the way to being realized, a pursuit she continued until the end of her life. "Moving from silence into speech is for the oppressed, the colonized, the exploited, and those who stand and struggle side by side a gesture of defiance that makes new life and new growth possible. It is that act of speech, of 'talking back,' that is no mere gesture of empty words, that is the expression of our movement from object to subject—the liberated voice." She continued to write until her passing, including a book with Cornel West, *Breaking Bread: Insurgent Black Intellectual Life*, and always challenged our preconceptions and prejudices.

> **"I was always saying the wrong thing,**
> **asking the wrong questions. I could not**
> **confine my speech to the necessary**
> **corners and concerns of my life."**
>
> **—bell hooks,**
> American author, professor, feminist, and social activist

GWENDOLYN BROOKS:
Poet of the Beat

Gwendolyn Brooks is one of the most innovative poets in the literary pantheon of America. Born in 1917 in Topeka, Kansas, her family moved when she was young to the far more urban city of Chicago, a street-smart influence that informed her work. Brooks wanted to bring poetry to the poor Black kids of the inner city. She did—rapid fire, tightly wound iambic pentameter that predated rap and won her the distinction of being the first Black person to receive the Pulitzer Prize (for *Annie Allen* in 1950). In later life, she took a more radical bent, hooking up with revolutionary Black Beat LeRoi Jones (now Amiri Baraka) and Don L. Lee and jumping into the causes of African Americans with both feet. She became a tough and angry Black Power poet penning verses grounded in classical style deconstructed through the lens of her newfound racial awareness and commitment to cause. Decades after her prizewinning feat, her poetry is still raw, fresh, and commanding.

> **"I want to clarify my language. I want these poems to be free. I want them to be directed without sacrificing the kind of music, the picture-making I've always been interested in."**
>
> **—Gwendolyn Brooks,**
>
> poet and teacher who earned more than fifty honorary degrees during her career

AUDRE LORDE:
A Burst of Life

Poet and activist **Audre Lorde** made the journey from literary obscurity to iconic status and widespread recognition without ever compromising what she had to say. A Black lesbian poet who never hid her truth, she started writing poetry seriously in grade school. Born in the winter of 1934, her parents were West Indian immigrants who escaped to New York City from Grenada in 1924, just in time for the Great Depression. Lorde grew up with a sense of being different from her two older sisters, feeling like she was really an only child or "an only planet, or some isolated world in a hostile, or at best, unfriendly firmament."

Dazzlingly bright, Lorde read voraciously. After a stint at the University of Mexico, where the atmosphere of racial tolerance really opened her eyes to the racism in the United States, she began attending Hunter College and earned a degree in library science from Columbia. Married with two small children, she worked for several New York libraries for eight years. Divorcing, she again moved toward her true passion—creative writing, both prose and poetry. In 1968, she started teaching creative writing at City University of New York. She also spent a year as poet in residence at Tougaloo College in Jackson, Mississippi, and went on to teach at many prestigious schools throughout America, where her reputation as an extraordinarily gifted poet grew.

Exemplifying the rare combination of gifted writer *and* teacher, Audre Lorde challenged her students. According to biographer Joanne S. Richmond in *Handbook of American Women's History*, Lorde urged her writing students to "Claim every aspect of themselves and encourage(d) them to discover the power of a spirited wholeness, knowing that in silence there is no growth, in suppression there is no personal satisfaction."

Her prose includes *The Cancer Journals,* disclosing her battle with breast cancer, from which she ultimately died. Lorde, who encountered a feminist's nightmare in her treatment, refused to wear the prosthetic breast her doctor tried to force upon her. In 1982, *Ami: a New Spelling of My Name* was Lorde's foray into creating a new genre she called "biomythology," as well as her literary outing of her own lesbianism. In *Ami*, she digs deep into archetype, myth, and women's mysteries through the story of her

FEMALE, GIFTED & BLACK

mother's birthplace, the island of Carriacou in the West Indies. Lorde reveled in the lore of African goddesses and matriarchal tales, in tales of her lusty lovemaking with other Black women, and in the intrinsic egalitarianism of nature. A staunch feminist and political activist, in her work she also pointed to the patriarchal "I" centeredness of Judeo-Christian traditions and confronted the hypocrisy of her times, angrily decrying sexism and bigotry in such poems as "Cables to Rage" and "The Black Unicorn."

On many occasions, Lorde read her poetry with fellow Black poets Amiri Baraka, Nikki Giovanni, and Jayne Cortez. She began, as many poets do, in coffeehouses and humble church basements. But soon she was filling theaters and winning awards, including the American Book Award for *A Burst of Light*, a nomination for the 1974 National Book Award in poetry, and the Walt Whitman Citation of Merit, for which she became New York's Poet Laureate shortly before losing her life to cancer in 1992.

Audre Lorde is a poet's poet. Scratch the surface of many of today's best writers' influences and her name will come up repeatedly. Jewelle Gomez cites Lorde as a major influence on her writing life and on the lives of many others in the African American creative community. In an article for *Essence* magazine, Gomez recognizes Lorde's work as "a mandate to move through...victimization and create independent standards that will help us live full and righteous lives...She was a figure all women could use as a grounding when they fought for recognition of their worth."

> **"Poetry is the conflict in the lives we lead. It is the most subversive because it is in the business of encouraging change."**
>
> **—Audre Lorde,**
> American author and activist; she wrote on the struggles of being Black, being a woman, and being a lesbian

WAR/AN /HIRE:
Telling Untold Stories of Those Caught in Conflict

Warsan Shire is a British poet, editor, and activist. She was born in 1988 in Kenya to Somali parents but grew up in London, England. She has a bachelor's degree in creative writing and was named poet in residence in Queensland, Australia, in 2014. Shire is the author of the collections *Teaching My Mother How to Give Birth* (2011), *Her Blue Body* (2015), and *Our Men Do Not Belong to Us* (2015). Her poems have appeared in the anthologies *Salt Book of Younger Poets* (2011), *Long Journeys: African Migrants on the Road* (2013), and *Poems That Make Grown Women Cry* (2016), and in the musical performer Beyoncé's visual album *Lemonade* (2016). According to *New Yorker* reviewer Alexis Okeowo, her work "embodies the kind of shapeshifting, culture-juggling spirit lurking in most people who can't trace their ancestors to their country's founding fathers, or whose ancestors look nothing like those fathers. In that limbo, Shire conjures up a new language for belonging and displacement." Her poems tie together gender, sex, war, and the interplay of differing cultural beliefs. As a poet, she transforms the pain of exile and alienation.

Shire is the poetry editor of *Spook* magazine and has been a guest editor at *Young Sable LitMag*. She has read her work on three continents, and in 2013, she won Brunel University's inaugural African Poetry Prize. In 2014, she was named the first Young Poet Laureate of London, England; the next year, the editorial board of *The New York Times* quoted a passage from her eloquent poem "Home" in a piece asking the nations of the West to allow refugees more leeway in crossing borders and give them more aid:

> *you have to understand*
> *that no one puts their children in a boat*
> *unless the water is safer than the land*
>
> **—Warsan Shire,**
> "Home"

CLAUDIA RANKINE:
Confronting the Injustice of Racism

Claudia Rankine, born in Kingston, Jamaica, earned a bachelor's degree at Williams College and an MFA at Columbia University. She has published several collections of poetry, beginning with *Nothing in Nature is Private* (1994), which won the Cleveland State Poetry Prize, followed by *Don't Let Me Be Lonely: An American Lyric* (2004). In 2014, *Citizen: An American Lyric* won the National Book Critics Circle Award in Poetry, the PEN Center USA Poetry Award, and the Forward poetry prize.

Her work crosses genres; as critic Calvin Bedient observed, "Hers is an art neither of epiphany nor story.... Rankine's style is the sanity, but just barely, of the insanity; the grace, but just barely, of the grotesqueness." Her poems also appear in the anthologies *Great American Prose Poems: From Poe to the Present* (2003), *Best American Poetry* (2001), and *The Garden Thrives: Twentieth Century African-American Poetry* (1996). Her play *Detour/South Bronx* premiered in 2009 at the Foundry Theater in New York. Rankine also coedited *American Women Poets in the 21st Century: Where Lyric Meets Language* (2002), *American Poets in the 21st Century: The New Poetics* (2007), and *The Racial Imaginary: Writers on Race in the Life of the Mind* (2014). Rankine has received fellowships from the MacArthur Foundation, the Academy of American Poets, the National Endowment for the Arts, the Lannan Foundation, and the Guggenheim Foundation. She was elected a chancellor of the Academy of American Poets in 2013, and in 2014, she won a Lannan Literary Award. She has taught at Barnard College, Case Western Reserve University, Pomona College, and the University of Houston.

Poets are not the only innovators of language. Playwrights also lend their ears to their work, bringing convincing dialogue and drama to the stage. Black women playwrights tackle all the hard issues: racism, sexism, and domestic intrigue among them. Here are just a few of the many Black women who have made their mark in the theater.

LORRAINE HAN/BERRY:
Young, Gifted, and Black

Chicago native **Lorraine Hansberry** was born in 1930 to a politically aware and progressive family who knew they had to work to make the changes they wished to see. But they paid a price. When she was only five, Hansberry was given a white fur coat for Christmas but was beaten up when she wore it to school. In 1938, the Black family moved to Hyde Park, an exclusive and exclusively white neighborhood. Hansberry's first memories of living in that house are of violence—being spit on, cursed at, and having bricks thrown through the windows. Her mother Nannie kept a gun inside the house in case it got any worse. An Illinois court evicted them, but her real estate broker father hired NAACP attorneys and had the decision overturned at the Supreme Court level, winning a landmark victory in 1940. He died at a relatively young age, which Hansberry ascribed to the pressure of the long struggle for civil rights.

Hansberry's parents' work as activists brought them into contact with the Black leaders of the day. She was well accustomed to seeing luminaries such as Langston Hughes, Paul Robeson, and W.E.B. DuBois in her home. Educated in the segregated public schools of the time, she attended the University of Wisconsin at Madison before she moved to New York for "an education of another kind."

Throughout her life, she remained dedicated to the values her parents had instilled in her and worked steadfastly for the betterment of Black people. At a picket line protesting the exclusion of Black athletes from college sports, Hansberry met the man she would marry, a white Jewish liberal, Robert Nemiroff. She worked for Paul Robeson's radical Black newspaper *Freedom* until her husband's career as a musician and songwriter earned enough to support them so that she could write full-time.

Her first play, *A Raisin in the Sun*, was a huge hit, winning the New York Drama Critics' Circle Award as Best Play of the Year in 1959. Hansberry was the youngest American and the first Black person to receive this prize. This proved to be a watershed event; after the success of *A Raisin in the Sun*, Black actors and writers entered the creative arts in a surge. Hansberry continued to write plays, but in 1963 was diagnosed with cancer. She died six years after winning the Drama Critics' Award at the age of thirty-four, tragically cutting short her work. Nevertheless, she made huge strides with her play, forever changing "the Great White Way."

> **"Racism is a device that, of itself, explained nothing. It is simply a means, an invention to justify the rule of some men over others."**
>
> **—from *Les Blancs: The Collected Last Plays of Lorraine Hansberry***

M.J. FIEVRE:
The Badass Black Girl

Born in Port-au-Prince, Haiti, **M.J. Fievre** currently writes from Winter Garden, Florida. M.J.'s publishing career began as a teenager in Haiti, a country that is both beautiful and violent. M.J. experienced that violence at an early age as she witnessed the political chaos unfolding around her. Her home life was also plagued by domestic violence. Her first mystery novel, *Le Feu de la Vengeance*, was published at the age of sixteen. At nineteen, she signed her first book contract with Hachette-Deschamps, in Haiti, for the publication of a young adult book titled *La Statuette Maléfique*. To date, M.J. has authored nine books in French that are widely read in Europe and the French Antilles.

Her plays have been performed at the Miami MicroTheater and at the O, Miami Festival's Poetry Press Week. In 2019, Mango Publishing released her book *Happy, Okay?*, a poem in play format. *Happy, Okay?* explores the topics of depression and anxiety. M.J. views writing as an emotional survival tool and works with other writers to tell their stories as a form of therapy, activism, and healing, whether they know they need it or not. She is also the author of the bestselling Badass Black Girl series of books, nonfiction self-empowerment guides for young Black women.

Poetry and drama go hand in hand. Both genres use voices as a means of expression. Poets use the poetic voice; playwrights create convincing dialogue that is often poetic in nature. Here are more poets and playwrights you should explore.

- When an angry group of white men burned down her father's store in Baltimore, Maryland, **Marian X** was placed in foster care. At age fifteen, she got involved with the NAACP and learned about nonviolent protest. In addition to plays, she writes fiction, nonfiction, and poetry.

- **Mahogany Browne** coordinated a Women of the World poetry slam to highlight women's voices. Her *Black Girl Magic* spoken word takes the listeners on a journey from the predefined stereotypes that Black girls are expected to fulfill to the strength, poise, and beauty Black girls can embody.

- Poet, author, and empowerment writer **Stephanie Lahart** has written books to encourage and uplift women to know and love themselves.

- African American poet, writer, and dramatist **Mari Evans** was not only known for creating written work with themes that were extremely influential in the culture of the 1950s and 1960s but also for creating, producing, writing, and directing a TV show in Indiana called *The Black Experience*, in which Evans hoped to reflect the Black community in such a way as to allow African Americans to see themselves and their experiences represented. The weekly show aired for five years, from 1968 to 1973. Evans lived to the ripe old age of ninety-seven and was the last surviving poet of the Black Arts Movement until she passed away in 2017.

- Afro-Dominican American poet **Elizabeth Acevedo** won a Carnegie Medal for her first book, *The Poet X*. In a world where being a self-contained island is overvalued, she believes that by slowing down and by being present, we can each individually make an impression on someone for good.

- Poet, writer, and attorney **M. NourbeSe Philip** left a promising career as a lawyer to become a full-time writer. She has created a new form of poetry called legal poetry, and her first book is used in education in high school classrooms all over Ontario.

- Poet, writer, activist, and educator **Aja Monet** was the first, the only, and the youngest woman to win the Nuyorican Poets Café Grand Slam title. Since then, she has used her voice to speak against police brutality, highlighting how it harms Black women.

- American playwright, poet, and feminist **Ntozake Shange** fell for poetry at a young age. Her most notable piece, *For Colored Girls Who Have Considered Suicide/When the Rainbow Is Enuf*, had a two-year run on Broadway from 1976–1978, and a revival production ran on Broadway in 2022.

- **June Jordan** is a Jamaican American self-identified bisexual, poet, essayist, teacher, and activist who began writing at the age of seven. In a time when being bisexual was considered abhorrent, she refused to deny her relational preference and identity and went on to write prominent pieces that delved into race, class, sexuality, and political activism.

- **Marita Bonner**, a writer, essayist, and playwright who is commonly associated with the Harlem Renaissance, encouraged African Americans to use knowledge, teaching, and writing to overcome inequalities.

- One of the earliest female African American playwrights, **Georgia Douglas Johnson** was an important figure from the Harlem Renaissance who played a big part in the anti-lynching movement and used her plays to talk about the realities of lynching.

- **Lucille Clifton** humanized her subjects with her writing and raised awareness of the everyday lives of African American people. As her poems highlighted the Black experience, other races were able to identify with her words, catalyzing necessary dialogues. Discovered by Langston Hughes, she was a prolific, prizewinning, and widely respected poet.

- **Marilyn Nelson** (*Abba Jacob and Miracles*) began writing in elementary school. The first poem she ever wrote was to honor her little brother who had passed away. She grew up and went on to win the Ruth Lilly Poetry Prize, the NSK Neustadt Prize for Children's Literature, and the Frost Medal.

- Abolitionist, poet, and activist **Frances Ellen Watkins Harper** published her first book of poems at the age of twenty-one. She spent any free time she had reading or writing.

- Former US Poet Laureate **Natasha Tretheway**'s book *Domestic Work* explores the lives and jobs of working-class Black men and women in the South.

- **Luffina Lourduraj** remarkably wrote, "She sacrifices her dreams to make my dream come true," portraying the self-sacrificing love of a mother.

- **Michelle Cliff** wrote mainly on the different aspects enveloping her multicultural identity: "Freedom without the means to be self-supporting is a one-armed triumph."

- National Book Award finalist **Patricia Smith** is an American poet, spoken word performer, playwright, author, and teacher who fell in love with poetry because there was nothing left to hide behind while performing on the spoken word stage. Her book *Blood Dazzler* is written in the voices of Hurricane Katrina victims.

- In addition to having published several collections, including *Somewhere in Advance of Nowhere* and *Mouth on Paper,* **Jayne Cortez** performs with her band, the Firespitters.

- **Tracy K. Smith** is a poet and educator who served as the twenty-second Poet Laureate from 2017 to 2019.

- **Ashley M. Jones** is the youngest person ever to be named poet laureate of Alabama. She is also the first Black poet laureate of Alabama. Her latest collection is *Reparations Now!* She is the sister of Monique L. Jones, author of *The Book of Awesome Black Americans*.

- American poet **Sonia Sanchez** is the author of more than sixteen books. She was active in the Civil Rights

Movement and is also the recipient of numerous literary awards, including the 2022 Barnes & Noble Writers for Writers Award.

- American poet **Wanda Coleman** has authored twenty books. Her poetry deals with racism and the consequences of living below the poverty line in Los Angeles.

ELIZABETH ALEXANDER:
She Had a Dream

Elizabeth Alexander is an American poet, essayist, and playwright; since 2018, she is also the president of the Andrew W. Mellon Foundation. She was born in Harlem, New York City in 1962 but grew up in Washington, DC. She was only a toddler when her parents took her to the March on Washington to hear Dr. Martin Luther King Jr. make his renowned "I Have a Dream" speech calling for an end to racism on August 28, 1963. The purpose of the march, which was one of the largest civil rights marches in American history, was to raise awareness about racial issues and advocate for the civil and economic rights of Black people. Estimates numbered the crowd size at about 250,000. The march is credited with helping the Civil Rights Act pass in Congress in 1964.

Alexander earned a bachelor's degree at Yale University, a master's degree at Boston University, and went on to complete her PhD at the University of Pennsylvania in 1992. While she was working toward her PhD, she also taught college classes. Her first book, *The Venus Hottentot*, was published in 1990 and won widespread praise from reviewers. The title of the book comes from a nickname for a Black woman named Saartjie Baartman who was exhibited in London and Paris. Horrifyingly, she was later dissected and preserved for public view. Alexander has released eight collections of poetry, most dealing with Blackness, history, and memory. She taught African American studies at Yale University and has chaired the department since 2008. On January 20, 2009, she recited her poem "Praise Song for the Day" at the inauguration of Barack Obama. Alexander has won numerous prizes for her work. She wrote, "...[N]ow I know my capacity for awe is infinite: This thirst is permanent, the well bottomless, my good fortune vast."

SYLVIA MOY:
The Song Poet

Lyricists (or "song poets") write the lyrics to original music, add lyrics to existing music, or compose lyrics for a cappella pieces. The lyrics of Aretha Franklin, Ella Fitzgerald, Bessie (Mamie) Smith, and Billie Holiday fit particular styles of music in accord with particular vocal qualities of each artist, along with the genre, theme, length, and rhythm of each song. Songwriters, composers, arrangers, and other musical artists often collaborate with lyricists; lyrics give songs substance and content. Lyricists can use words in a way that complements the music, makes a song memorable, and captures the listener's attention.

Sylvia Rose Moy was born in 1938 in Detroit, Michigan, and grew up with eight siblings in the northeast side of the city. Moy told the *Detroit Free Press* that the children, who had "music in their bloodlines on both sides," kept themselves entertained with pots and pans. In addition to playing the piano on the radiator, Moy made musical instruments out of food boxes. Moy revealed in an interview with Adam White, who wrote the book *Motown: The Sound of Young America* (2016), that her father Melvin, an appliance repairman, and her mother, née Hazel Redgell, a homemaker, were the inspirations for "I Was Made to Love Her."

At Northern High School, she studied jazz and classical music. After graduation, she traveled to New York City to promote her songs, but found no buyers. A rejection from a record company executive haunted her for years. "You don't have a bad voice," the executive told her, "but you will never be a songwriter." (Years later, the same executive tried to buy out her songwriting contract at Motown Records.) In 1963, after Marvin Gaye and Mickey Stevenson saw her perform at Detroit's Caucus Club, she was invited to Motown's West Grand Boulevard complex. She was shocked when Motown offered her a recording contract, a management contract, and a songwriter's contract, as she told the *Free Press* in 2016. However, songwriting would take precedence over singing if she was hired as the company was short on material for its existing artists. She agreed to this condition and became a songwriter. The hit machine got into gear and started rolling.

The company was worried about the future of Stevie Wonder's career when Sylvia Moy joined Motown in 1964. The thirteen-year-old prodigy's first single, "Fingertips Pt. 2," had reached Number 1 on the *Billboard* Hot 100 and R&B charts a year earlier. His subsequent recordings were not as successful, and Motown executives were uncertain what to do with him as he grew into an adult. Stevie's voice was different, and they weren't sure how to handle it. He hadn't been selling well for a while, and it was becoming possible the label would let him go. Moy begged Mickey Stevenson, head of artists and repertoire at Motown, to allow her to work with Mr. Wonder; together they would write a hit. "Let this be my task," Moy told Stevenson. She believed in Wonder, affirming, "I don't believe it's over for him."

Wonder played Moy some of the "ditties" he had been working on, but none of them sounded great. As she was leaving, he played her one final piece of music and sang, "Baby, everything is all right." There wasn't much more to it yet, he said, and Moy told him she would take it home and work on the melody and lyrics. Henry "Hank" Cosby, a Motown producer, assisted in the writing of "Uptight." Unfortunately, there was

no Braille transcription of the lyrics for Wonder to read in the recording studio. As he recorded, Moy sang the lyrics through his earphones, one line ahead. *Billboard*'s Hot 100 ranked "Uptight" No. 3 on the pop chart, and the single topped the R&B chart.

With the song's success, Moy had earned a spot on the label's creative team. In addition to those songs, she collaborated with Wonder and Cosby on "My Cherie Amour" (1969), "Nothing's Too Good for My Baby" (1966), and "I Was Made to Love Her" (1967), which featured Stevie Wonder's mother, Lula Mae Hardaway, as a cowriter. Wonder's title for "My Cherie Amour" had been "Oh, My Marcia," but Moy gave it a French twist. As their work together has unfolded, she is now best known for the songs she wrote with and for Stevie Wonder.

Moy also wrote "Honey Chile" and "Love Bug Leave My Heart Alone" by Martha and the Vandellas. With Lamont Dozier and Brian and Eddie Holland, one of Motown's most prolific songwriting teams, Moy cowrote "This Old Heart of Mine (Is Weak for You)," which hit No. 12 on the charts for the Isley Brothers in 1966. "It Takes Two," which she cowrote with William "Mickey" Stevenson for Marvin Gaye and Kim Weston, reached No. 14 on the Hot 100 in 1967. She was the first woman at the label to bear the job title of "record producer," and one of the busiest and most well-known songwriters of the time. She also wrote theme songs for several television shows and movies and eventually received six Grammy nominations.

She was inducted into the Songwriters Hall of Fame alongside fellow Motown songwriter and producer Hank Cosby in 2006; on that day, Stevie Wonder made a surprise appearance at the ceremony to perform "Uptight" for his former collaborator. In an interview afterward, he praised her for "[finding] unique ways to take the melodies I wrote and putting them into a lyric that was incredible and that touched many hearts."

In addition to writing 180 songs, Moy won twenty BMI Awards, including three for "Honey Chile," "I Was Made to Love Her," and "Shoo-Be-Doo-Be-Doo-Da-Day." She left Motown in 1973 when the company moved to Los Angeles and went on to sign with 20th Century Records as a songwriter, singer, and producer. Additionally, she mentored young people interested in the arts. As cofounder of the Center for Creative Communications, commonly known as "Masterworks," she invested heavily in the future of the arts by working with underprivileged children in Detroit. Young adults are trained at the Center in telecommunications and media arts. Her Masterpiece Studios, on Detroit's west side, has attracted artists like Kem.

_____

Despite stereotyping admonishments that "women don't produce," many Black women hold their own as lyricists, songwriters, recording artists, and in-demand producers.

VALERIE SIMPSON:
The Talented Duo

Valerie Simpson has long been known as half of the legendary duo Ashford & Simpson. Simpson and her now departed husband Nickolas Ashford wrote and produced many popular pop and R&B songs, including "I'm Every Woman" (a hit for Chaka Khan and Whitney Houston) and "Ain't No Mountain High Enough" (a hit for Marvin Gaye & Tammi Terrell, and for Diana Ross). Ashford and Simpson's music has been featured in international events such as the opening of the Olympics and the Hands Across America theme "Reach Out and Touch Somebody." Ashford and Simpson created a catalog of chart-topping hit singles and albums that is unparalleled in today's music industry. The pair received many awards and honors over the years. In 1996, they received ASCAP's highest honor, the Founders Award. The duo also received the Rhythm and Blues Foundation Pioneer Award in 1999, and in 2002, they were inducted into the Songwriters Hall of Fame. After Ashford's death in 2011, Valerie Simpson continued to be active as a songwriter and artist, releasing a solo album called *Dinosaurs Are Coming Back Again* in 2012, and she continues to write and perform live.

MISSY ELLIOTT:
One in a Million

Born in 1971 in Portsmouth, Virginia, **Missy Elliott** had a traumatic childhood. She formed the girl group Fayze, writing most of the songs and enlisting Timbaland (Tim Mosley) to produce. After impressing Jodeci's DeVante Swing, she and the group moved to New York, changed their name to Sista, and signed to Elektra Records on DeVante's Swing Mob imprint. In 1993, she wrote (and rapped on) her first hit, "That's What Little Girls Are Made Of," for Raven-Symoné. She fronted Sista's single "Brand New" in 1994, then worked on tracks for Aaliyah. Her Top 10 hits include "Hot Boyz," "Lose Control," "Get Ur Freak On," "Gossip Folks," and "Work It," which won the Grammy Award for Best Female Rap Solo Performance and MTV's Video of the Year award in 2004. Her groundbreaking songs, focusing on feminism, gender equality, body positivity, and sex positivity, paved the way for artists such as Destiny's Child, Eve, Macy Gray, Beyoncé, and Nicki Minaj.

MAHALIA JACKSON:
The Queen of Gospel

Mahalia Jackson was born in 1911 in New Orleans, Louisiana. She is widely considered one of the most influential singers of this century and was also a talented lyricist. Despite racial segregation, which pervaded American society during her lifetime, she achieved substantial and unexpected success in her recording career, selling an estimated 22 million records and performing in front of integrated secular as well as gospel audiences around the world.

Jackson was a granddaughter of enslaved people. At birth, she had bowed legs and infections in both her eyes. Her eyes recovered quickly, but she was nicknamed "Fishhooks" because of the curvature in her legs. However, young Mahalia's legs began to straighten on their own when she was in her teens. Music was everywhere in New Orleans, with the sound of blues often pouring out of neighboring houses. She was also intrigued by "second line" funeral procession musicians playing brisk jazz as they returned from cemeteries. Already blessed with a powerful voice, at age twelve, she joined the junior choir. Her father's church taught her gospel singing during her upbringing, which led to her lifelong dedication to proclaiming God's word through song.

Blues singers Bessie Smith and Jelly Roll Morton inspired Jackson. She later moved to Chicago to join the Johnson Singers, one of the first gospel groups. She became the first gospel recording artist to tour Europe in 1947 with the release of the acclaimed "Move On Up a Little Higher," which sold over two million copies, making it the bestselling gospel single in history. During the Civil Rights Movement, she sang at the March on Washington at the request of Dr. Martin Luther King Jr. Some of her other most popular performances and songs include "Precious Lord" (1956),

"Just A Closer Walk With Thee" (1966), and "Down By The Riverside" (1956).

She faced intense pressure throughout her career to record secular music but turned down high paying opportunities to focus on gospel. Since she frequently credited elements of Black culture in the development of her style, such as slavery songs she had heard in churches, work songs sung by vendors on the streets of New Orleans, and blues and jazz bands, the success of the "Queen of Gospel" made the Black community proud.

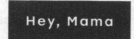

Hey, Mama

Many people don't realize that many lyrics sang by famous male artists were written by Black women. (Mind blown!)

Lizzie Douglas, better known as **Memphis Minnie** (1897–1973), cowrote Led Zeppelin's "When the Levee Breaks." She was a blues guitarist, singer, and songwriter whose career spanned over three decades. Her best-known songs include "When the Levee Breaks," "Me and My Chauffeur Blues," "Bumble Bee," and "Nothing in Rambling." Minnie's gravestone reads: "The hundreds of sides Minnie recorded are the perfect material to teach us about the blues. For the blues are at once general and particular—speaking for millions, but in a highly singular, individual voice. Listening to Minnie's songs, we hear her fantasies, her dreams, her desires, but we will hear them as if they were our own."

Brittany Talia Hazzard, better known as **Starrah,** cowrote "Wasted Times" by The Weeknd and "Girls Like You" by Maroon 5. Growing up in Delaware, she was the youngest out of nine children in her family. Her lyrics describe the police raids she experienced as a child growing up in the ghetto. Her songwriting evolved from writing short stories and poems. She was sometimes rejected from studio sessions for being "too urban" in her early career, but she later found success crossing over from the urban genre into mainstream pop music. Several songs she has written or cowritten have reached the Top 20 on the US *Billboard* Hot 100, and three of the songs she's cowritten have reached number one. One of those #1 tracks won her the Grammy Award for Best Rap Song in 2020: "Savage Remix," recorded and performed by Megan Thee Stallion with Beyoncé. Additionally, she collaborated on Travis Scott's *Birds in the Trap Sing McKnight* and contributed five songs to Calvin Harris's *Funk Wav Bounces Vol. 1,* including the Top 20 single "Feels" featuring Pharrell Williams, Katy Perry, and Big Sean.

Andrea Martin, who cowrote the song "You're the One" for the all-female group SWV, also wrote songs for Toni Braxton, Leona Lewis, Melanie Fiona, Sean Kingston, Fantasia Barrino, and Jennifer Hudson. Andrea graduated from New York City's LaGuardia High School of Music & Art and Performing Arts in 1990 with a major in vocal music; clearly her talents were not limited to songwriting. A promising singer, in 1998, she released an album, *The Best of Me.* In a panel discussion at the 2011 ASCAP Expo, Martin discussed the importance of speaking from the heart when making music: "Sing from the heart. I don't care if it's rock, country or whatever, the best records come from the heart," she said. "It's okay to go in the booth and just freestyle."

The production and songwriting team **Nova Wav** consists of Brittany "Chi" Coney and Denisia "Blu June" Andrews. They famously cowrote "Stick Around" with Lukas Graham, and most recently, collaborated with Beyoncé on her seventh solo album *Renaissance*. Other artists for whom the duo has written and produced tracks include Rihanna, DJ Khaled, Ariana Grande, Jay-Z, Saweetie, Nicki Minaj, Teyana Taylor, Kehlani, and more. In 2018, *Billboard* included Nova Wav in its list of 100 R&B/Hip-Hop Power Players.

Esther Renay Dean is an American singer, songwriter, and actress who has earned the name "The Song Factory": She cowrote David Guetta's "Hey Mama," one of a total of more than a dozen Top 10 songs, including No. 1 hits for Rihanna and Katy Perry. She was nominated for Album of the Year at the 54th Annual Grammy Awards for producing Rihanna's album *Loud*. Dean made her acting debut in the film *Pitch Perfect* (2012), and reprised the role in *Pitch Perfect 2* (2015) and *Pitch Perfect 3* (2017). She also voiced two of the characters in *Ice Age: Continental Drift*, the fourth film in the Ice Age series, and wrote a song for the film, "We Are (Family)."

Other lyricists of note include Black women who have worked with major artists like Beyoncé or Jennifer Lopez:

- **Makeba Riddick-Woods,** also known as "Girl Wonder."
- **Carla Marie Williams**, a woman who inspires in the worlds of both music and social change, founded

Girls I Rate to push for gender equality, create opportunities, and empowering young women in the music and entertainment industries.

- **Christina Milian** broke through at the tender age of nineteen, dropping several international hit singles on her debut album with Murder Inc. Records. She lost no time getting into acting as well, appearing in several films including *Love Don't Cost a Thing*, as well as the TV sitcom *Grandfathered* (2015-2016). She and her family were featured in the 2015 reality series *Christina Milian Turned Up*.

- **Diana Gordon,** the "secret ingredient in Beyoncé's Lemonade."

- The incomparable **Mariah Carey**, known as the "Songbird Supreme" and the "Queen of Christmas."

Herstory is richer because of the contributions of Black women in the genres of theater, music, and poetry. Whether the stage they are storming is a national one or one that is off-off-Broadway, the contributions these women have made in the arts serve to expand our perspective. They bring untold stories to life, chronicling a long and challenging past; they embody ideals that are worthy of honor and champion civil rights with their writing.

chapter four

WHAT THE EYE SEES

BLACK FEMALE VISUAL ARTISTS

Throughout history, with rooms of their own or not, Black women have written, painted, danced, composed, and turned their photographic eyes on the world, expressing both feelings and artistic visions in their works. The impact of these artistic women on our culture has been Incredible. Their sphere of influence is the globe we inhabit!

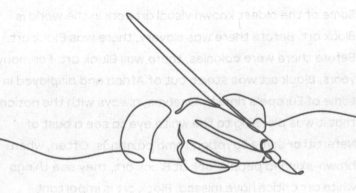

Fearless creativity and relentless pursuit of artistic truth on the part of these sheroes have freed the imagination to its limitless bounds. They have produced art that shocks, and poetry that pierces, created new ritual dances, designated fantastic fashions, and looked into the very heart of the darkness that is the feminine. The lives of these women suggest that real inspiration can come only from being true to yourself at any cost.

Black women artists create through sheer ingenuity. Concept becomes reality. Imagination becomes solidified. Often Black female artists address matters of import in their works, creating vital commentaries on society and the injustices they have faced throughout history. Black art *is* history. Whether it is **Betye Saar**'s work in the medium known as assemblage or **Augusta Savage**'s sculptures, most of the time, Black art has a story to tell to those who are willing to listen.

_____

Some of the oldest known visual artwork in the world is Black art. Before there was slavery, there was Black art. Before there were colonies, there was Black art. For many years, Black art was stolen out of Africa and displayed in some of Europe's finest museums, always with the notion that it was pleasing to the white eye to see a bust of Nefertiti or some Egyptian tomb paintings. Often, when brown-skinned people look at Black art, they see things white art critics have missed. Black art is important because it opens art to a wide spectrum of skin colors that ranges far beyond white and shows us different perspectives on reality.

It is next to impossible to define Black art because it is multifaceted and dynamic. There is no one thing that encapsulates Black art. Black art is powerful, and it is unique in its forms. Black art is also history, and it is often a chronicle of struggles for liberation. Whether it was the quiltmakers who hid secret messages in the designs of their quilts during the years when it was illegal for slaves to read and write or field workers singing in harmony under the hot sun, nothing stopped Black artists from creating art for long. There is strength in numbers, and the best of Black art has often been created in the context of movements that supported and nurtured artists, including the Harlem Renaissance of the early twentieth century or the many movements and collectives that began to emerge during the 1960s, like AfriCOBRA, the Black Arts Movement, and Where We At. Black art flourishes when it is a collective endeavor, allowing artists to open doors that were long closed to them both as Black people and as women. It is no coincidence that Black arts movements are tied in with civil rights movements. When people express opposition and resistance to the way they've been treated, it leads to greater liberation from oppression and furthers the dismantling of racist ideas. Black art is a manifestation of pride in Black creativity and culture.

AUGUSTA SAVAGE:
The Most Original

Augusta Savage was an American sculptor and teacher most closely associated with the Harlem Renaissance. She was born in 1892 in Green Cove Springs, Florida, the daughter of a Methodist minister. From a very early age, Savage began making figures out of the red clay found in the ground near her home. Her father was opposed to her creative efforts and beat her regularly because he thought making these figures was sinful. But Savage didn't give up. When her family moved to West Palm Beach, Florida, in 1915, her high school teacher took notice of her talent as a sculptor and allowed her to teach a clay modeling class; this early experience led to a lifelong love of teaching.

In 1919, she won $25 at an arts festival in West Palm Beach for the most original exhibit. She moved to New York City in 1921 and attended Cooper Union on a scholarship, beating out 142 men who were on the waiting list, and graduated from its four-year program in three years. In 1923, Savage applied for a summer program at the Fountainebleau School of Fine Arts in France. She was selected for the program, but when the directors found out she was Black, they took back their offer, fearing that white students would be offended. Savage fought back against their decision but couldn't get the committee in charge to change its mind. This incident was covered by media on both sides of the Atlantic, and as a result, Savage was invited to study with the renowned sculptor Herman Atkins

MacNeil. This became the first of many battles Savage would wage for equal rights in her life. She studied in France until 1931, when she returned to Harlem. In 1934, she became the first Black woman in the National Association of Women Painters and Sculptors. She opened a community arts studio in a basement in Harlem; this resource she created for artists later became the Harlem Community Art Center. She also cofounded the Harlem Artists Guild. She was known for sculpting realistic images of Black Americans rather than relying on stereotypes. While she never sold many of her works, she was very popular in the Black arts community. Augusta Savage died of cancer in 1962. She said of her life, "From the time I can first recall the rain falling on the red clay in Florida, I wanted to make things."

Older Even Than Written Language

Mixed-media art is a type of art in which more than one material is used. For example, if you paint with watercolors and then add highlights with colored pencils, you are creating mixed-media art. Assemblages and collages are two specific genres of mixed-media artwork because artists often utilize a variety of found objects in creating their art. Multimedia art is like mixed-media art in that it uses more than one material and/or technique to create a piece, but it also often incorporates performing arts such as dance or music into the artwork for live performances and installations. Here are some of the most brilliant and multifaceted mixed-media mavens:

- **Betye Saar** is an American artist known for her work in the medium of assemblage. As a child, Saar collected and repaired small objects. She fell in love with art in graduate school. She started out as a printmaker, but soon began collecting racist images that she assembled into boxes with messages of power and strength of Black people. Her most famous work, *The Liberation of Aunt Jemima*, shows Aunt Jemima holding a rifle and a hand grenade.

- **Janet Taylor Pickett** is an American mixed-media artist. The myriad techniques she employs in creating her artwork include sculpting, installations, painting, assemblage, and collage. Vice President Kamala Harris collects Pickett's work and has a piece of her art in her Washington, DC, office. Pickett's work has been exhibited at the Museum of Modern Art in New York City, the Montclair Art Museum in New Jersey, and the Phillips Collection in Washington, DC.

- **Toyin Ojih Odutola** (born 1985) is a Nigerian American multimedia artist known for her vibrant drawings and works on paper. Using intricate marks and lavish compositions, she rethinks the genre and traditions of portraiture and storytelling. Ojih Odutola's artistic works frequently explore themes such as socioeconomic inequality, colonialism, queer theory, notions of Blackness as a visual and social symbol, and migration and dislocation.

- **Kay Brown** (1932–2012) was both an artist and a published author. She was the first woman to gain membership in the Harlem-based Weusi Artist Collective; founded in 1965, the collective was named after the Swahili word for "Blackness." The experience of being the only woman in the group prompted her to seek out ways to represent Black female artists. She is widely recognized as one of the founders of the Black women artists' collective Where We At in New York City. Using mixed-media collages and prints, Brown's works portray issues that affect the global Black community. The Brooklyn Museum exhibited Brown's work as part of their exhibit entitled "We Wanted a Revolution."

- Mixed-media artist **Delita Martin**'s works celebrate the complexity and strength of Black womanhood. On her vibrant canvases, her subjects appear amid floral and geometric patterns. Martin's portraits rely on a variety of materials and techniques, including charcoal, painting, and printmaking. She includes traditional West African motifs in her works, highlighting the resiliency of women.

- Throughout her career as an artist, **Monica Beasley** has explored themes such as feminism, femininity, home, marriage, family, race, and Southern culture. She works in a variety of media ranging from photography and conceptual art to painting and collage. The viewer is immediately drawn to the tactile materials and use of bright colors, yet each piece is deeply rooted in a serious subject.

- **Ruby Onyinyechi Amanze** is a Brooklyn-based Nigerian-British mixed-media artist; born in 1982, she held an early exhibition of her work in Nigeria after being recognized as a Fulbright scholar. Her work has gone on to be exhibited around the world, including in London, England, and South Africa. She focuses on the blurring of cultural identity and "post-colonial non-nationalism" in her work. Her drawings tell meandering tales of alien creatures who live in remarkable landscapes. Amanze believes that art, specifically drawing, has the power to communicate across cultural barriers, explaining, "The medium is classic. It's universal. It's as old as time, older even than written language. But at the same time, it's constantly reinventing itself and doing away with former parameters of what it could or could not be."

- **Ann "Sole Sister" Johnson**, who is primarily a mixed-media artist, has chronicled her exploration of racial issues, particularly in the Black community, in a series of evocative and engaging works such as *It Is the Not Knowing that Burns My Soul*, an investigation of exploratory mixed-media works examining Black Indian culture. The series was featured in an exhibition and catalog published by the Smithsonian's National Museum of the American Indian. Several of Johnson's works have been exhibited in solo, group, and juried exhibitions nationwide.

- Artist, art historian, and curator **Lavett Ballard** (born 1970) uses her artwork to reimagine the stories of people of African descent, with her primary focus placed on Black women's lives and history. She uses collaged photos embellished with paint, metallic foils, and oil pastels. She holds a dual bachelor's degree in art and art history from Rutgers University. In March of 2020, she was commissioned to create cover art for *TIME* magazine's Women of the Year issue. She was named one of the Top Ten Female Emerging Artists to Collect by Black Art in America and has exhibited her work across the United States.

Designing All the Spaces Inside

Let a creative Black woman inside your space and she will create a haven for you that is vibrant, provocative, and unique. Black designers are diverse in their style, and no one design strategy defines them, but they very often draw on African art and design elements, blending them with contemporary designs to create stunningly expressive works. Black interior designers and design strategists are increasing in popularity, and quite a number of them now have product lines that are available at one-stop shops like Target and Walmart, proving that there is a market for these smart women's designs. These Black female designers have left an indelible mark in interior design and design strategy:

Justina Blakeney is an interior designer and author. She has a design and lifestyle blog called *Jungalow*, with a name which combines the words "jungle" and "bungalow." She has had collections produced by Loloi, Hygge & West, Anthropologie, Target, Living Spaces, and Pottery Barn. She is author of *The New Bohemians*, a series of coffee-table books that provide interior design ideas along with project instructions.

Kesha Franklin is an American interior designer. Her interest in design began when she was a child as she thumbed through her father's collection of *Architectural Digest* and *GQ* magazines. In 2006, she founded the Beautiful Experience, a design firm that specializes in residential and commercial event production. She was a backstage production designer for Mercedes-Benz Fashion Week and is now the CEO and lead designer at Halden Interiors, an interior design firm that builds hospitality and residential spaces. She has been named a Designer to Watch by the Black Interior Designers Network and has been featured in

Dwell magazine, NBC's *Open House*, *Architectural Digest*, *Pro*, *Business of Home*, and *Array* magazine, among others.

American graphic designer and design strategist **Sylvia Harris** experienced racial discrimination firsthand while attending a desegregated high school. She described hearing her mother shout at Ku Klux Klan members who were parading in the streets. After later graduating from Yale University, she cofounded Two Twelve Associates and did design work for Citibank. In 1994, she left Two Twelve and opened Sylvia Harris LLC. Her focus at the new firm was on solving problems for civic agencies, hospitals, and universities. In 2014, she was awarded the American Institute of Graphic Arts medal. She was the creative director behind the design of the year 2000 US Census form. As she has said, "Design teaches us not to make assumptions."

Sheila Bridges is an American interior designer who opened her interior design firm, Sheila Bridges Design, in 1994. She has been named "America's Best Interior Designer" by CNN and *TIME* Magazine and has worked for many prominent clients including former president Bill Clinton, for whom she designed office space in Harlem, New York. Bridges has done interior design work for both Columbia and Princeton University. She is the author of two books, *Furnishing Forward: A Practical Guide to Furnishing for a Lifetime*, and *The Bald Mermaid: A Memoir*. Bridges has been featured in numerous magazines including *Architectural Digest*, *The New York Times*, *The Wall Street Journal*, *Interior Design*, and *House & Garden*. On television, she hosted four seasons of *Sheila Bridges Designer Living* for the Fine Living Network.

Her home furnishings are sold at Anthropologie and Bed Bath & Beyond, and her designs have been featured at museums all over the world, including the Smithsonian, the Museum of the City of New York, the Studio Museum in Harlem, the Museum of Art and Design in New York City, and the Museum of African American History and Culture in Washington, DC.

Uzo Njoku is a Nigerian American painter, pattern maker, and product designer. Born in Lagos, Nigeria, she immigrated to the United States with her mother when she was seven years old. Njoku initially wanted to study statistics, but after she painted the white walls of her home and posted the results on social media, her friends encouraged her to go into art. She began selling small paintings for $20 each and changed her major at the University of Virginia to studio art. Njoku then set out to design and publish her own coloring book, *The Bluestocking Society: A Coloring Book.* All of the images in the coloring book are of inspirational women of color such as Frida Kahlo and tennis legend Serena Williams.

From interior design, we'll step into the world of painting and take a look at Black women artists who have made a mark on the art world, one of whom was born on a pecan and cotton plantation. They used their painting skills to transport their viewers to imagined landscapes and scenes from history.

CLEMENTINE HUNTER:
Painting the Past While Reimagining the Future

Clementine Hunter was a self-taught Black artist known for her paintings. She was born near Cloutierville, Louisiana, in late December of 1886 or early January of 1887. The exact date of her birth is not known, but she was born close to Christmas on Hidden Hill Plantation, where cotton and pecan trees were cultivated. When she was five years old, her family moved to Cloutierville, where she attended a racially segregated school. Young Clementine found the school to be a harsh environment, and she left after a year of classroom study to go work in the cotton fields and pecan groves. She never learned to read or write and grew up speaking French Creole, only learning to speak English when she married in 1924. In the late 1920s, Hunter began working as a housekeeper at the Melrose plantation. The plantation became a gathering place for artists, and Hunter began formally painting in the late 1930s using discarded tubes of paint that visiting artists left behind. She was also a textile artist and produced many intricate quilts. She produced between 5,000 and 10,000 paintings in her lifetime and became recognized as a notable artist. Initially, her paintings sold for as little as twenty-five cents, but by the end of her life, her work was selling for thousands of dollars and was being displayed in museums all over the world. She was the first Black artist to have a solo exhibition at the New Orleans Museum of Art. In 1986,

Northwestern State University gave her an honorary Doctor of Fine Arts Degree.

History As Subject Matter

Silhouettists are artists who create silhouettes, images made by cutting out the outline of an object or person and then attaching it to a light or dark background for contrast. **Kara Walker** is best known for her silhouettes, which are room-sized black paper cut-outs on white backgrounds depicting the history of slavery and racism. She is the recipient of many awards, including the MacArthur Foundation Achievement Award and the Eileen Harris Norton Fellowship. She teaches visual arts at Rutgers University, and her work can be found in many museums, including the Guggenheim Museum, the Museum of Modern Art, the Metropolitan Museum of Art, and the Tate Gallery in London, as well as in private collections.

Tracy Murrell is a printmaker, collage artist, and painter. She is intrigued by the female figure and primarily creates silhouettes of Black women on colorful and dynamic backgrounds. Murrell uses ink, decorative papers, tile, resin, and high-gloss enamel in making her artwork. Through her artistic creations, she explores themes of identity, migration, and displacement.

AMY SHERALD:
Portraitist to First Ladies

A portraitist must develop certain necessary skills to be successful. They need to learn to draw or paint realistic images, including from memory, understand color theory, and use their imaginations to capture the essence and character of their subjects on canvas. For many years, portraits were only created for wealthy patrons and were mostly images of white people. Nowadays, many Black portraitists are creating paintings and images of Black people showcasing their diversity and accomplishments.

Amy Sherald was attracted to creating art from an early age and often skipped recess to draw. Despite her early interest in art, when she went to the Columbus Museum on a school field trip, she was stunned to discover that art could be a profession. Her parents, however, wanted her to become a doctor because it was a safer career than art. She enrolled as a pre-med student at Clark Atlanta University, but then switched her major to art after taking a painting class at Spelman College. She earned her Bachelor of Arts degree in painting in 1997 from Clark Atlanta University, then a Master of Fine Arts degree from the Maryland Institute College of Art.

During her early years as a painter, Sherald painted everyday Black people on the streets of Baltimore. It took her a long time to become a successful painter; she waited tables until she was thirty-eight years old, painting in her spare time. In 2016, she won the National Portrait Gallery's Outwin Boocher

Portrait Competition with her painting "Miss Everything (Unsuppressed Deliverances);" the prize came with a $25,000 award. The next year, she was selected to paint the official portrait of first lady Michelle Obama. Her portrait was unveiled along with Kehinde Wiley's portrait of Barack Obama in 2018. This made them the first two Black artists ever to paint official presidential portraits for the National Portrait Gallery. Her paintings are in many galleries around the world, including the US embassy in Dakar, Senegal, the National Museum of Women in the Arts in Washington, DC, the National Portrait Gallery in Washington, DC, and the National Museum of African American History and Culture in Washington, DC. "What was so shocking when I first went to a museum was to find out that art wasn't [just] something in a book or in an encyclopedia, that people did [art] a long time ago, that it was real life," she said. "And then, when I saw an image of a person of color, it all came together in that moment—that this was something real, that somebody created this who was alive at the same time that I was alive."

- During the Harlem Renaissance, **Laura Wheeler Waring** (1887–1948) was a popular portraitist whose favorite subjects included prominent African Americans; she taught art at Cheyney University in Pennsylvania for over three decades.
- In her portrait quilts, **Bisa Butler** depicts collectively experienced historical events as well as personal narratives of Black life. Textiles as an artistic medium

have traditionally been marginalized in the art world because of its association with women. Butler turns that on its head in her art, using the medium to interrogate the historical narratives of her subjects. Her work further brings us into the depth of her subjects by playing with subtle detail and scale in order to present them as complex, multifaceted individuals.

- The oil paintings of **Lynette Yiadom-Boakye** helped spark the renaissance of depicting the Black figure in art. Her subjects exist outside of the familiar realm of our everyday world, allowing each person who looks at them to draw on their own imagination to create context for what is seen, free of specified times and places or any set story.

- Painter **Genesis Tramaine** (born 1983) creates abstract portraits of figures who are not tied down by limitations of gender or race and transcend social structures. She is a queer-identified devotional artist inspired by Black congregations gathering at churches on Sunday mornings to sing gospel hymns in the spirit of fellowship. Tremaine utilizes the mundane to create both a spark of déjà vu and a visionary peek ahead at futures newly discovered by the viewer. Tremaine's style pays homage to the graffiti scene of New York City in the 1980s.

———

The first Black photographers began documenting Black life as early as 1840, the year after photography was invented and twenty-five years before slavery was abolished. While there were some white photographers who took realistic photographs of Black people, Black photographers took their cameras into their communities and documented life as they saw it, which was often in sharp contrast to the stereotypical images of Black people displayed in mainstream media outlets. Photography itself was important because it was an affordable means of having a portrait taken. Prior to the invention of photography, one would have to pay an artist to draw a portrait or paint an oil painting, a service far out of reach for many Black people. Black photographers have documented all the major historical events since the invention of photography, including the Civil War, the Harlem Renaissance, the Great Depression, both world wars, and the Civil Rights Movement. In creating their photographic images, photographers have also helped shape our history. Many Black photographers continue to document Black life in America: Photojournalists like **Coreen Simpson** have recorded images of many of the cultural icons of recent generations. **Carrie Mae Weems** creates photographs, films, and videos that provide social commentary on issues facing Black people in America, such as sexism and racism. **Dawoud Bey** creates large-scale photographs and street photography portraits of Black

FEMALE, GIFTED & BLACK

adolescents in their communities. **Deana Lawson**'s photographs portray the nuances of the experiences of Black Americans in relation to issues of social, political, and economic importance. **LaToya Ruby Frazier**'s photographs are a weapon for social justice, highlighting the effects of racism and environmental deterioration on individual people. And **Lorna Simpson**'s conceptual photography invites the viewer to dive deeply into issues of identity, gender, race, and history.

CARRIE MAE WEEMS:
Contemporary Art Influencer

Carrie Mae Weems is widely considered to be one of America's most influential contemporary artists. She explores many topics in her work, including family relationships, cultural identity, sexism, class, political systems, and the nature of power. Weems has been creating art for more than thirty years, utilizing photographs, text, fabric, audio, digital images, installations, and video. She has taken part in many group and solo exhibitions internationally at such esteemed venues as the Metropolitan Museum of Art, the Frist Art Museum, the Guggenheim Museum, and the Centro Andaluz de Arte Contemporáneo. In 2012, she received one of the first US State Department Medals of Arts in recognition for her commitment to their Art in Embassies program; the next year, she received the MacArthur Fellowship, known as the "Genius Grant." Weems has received the BET Honors Visual Artist award, the Lucie Award for Fine Art photography, the ICP Spotlights Award from the International Center of Photography, and the W.E.B. Du Bois Medal from Harvard University, and she was honored at the Guggenheim's 2014 International Gala. Institutions of art and learning including the California College of the Arts, Colgate University, Bowdoin College, the School of Visual Arts, and Syracuse University have all presented her with honorary degrees.

Along the Highways and Byways

Mary Ann Carroll was the first woman among the Florida Highwaymen, a group of twenty-six artists who painted Florida landscapes between the 1950s and 1980s, as well as the first woman to become the group's president. At the time, the painters were trying to make a living with their art rather than working on farms or in Florida citrus groves. They were shut out of traditional art galleries because they were Black and had no formal training. To sell their paintings, they'd put them in the trunk of one of their cars and go door-to-door, or else sell them along Florida's coastal highways, which is how their group got its name.

To make enough money to support themselves, the Highwaymen had to paint a little differently than gallery artists. Instead of canvases and frames, they used construction materials both to paint on and to frame their paintings. They also learned to paint quickly, producing as many as twenty-five paintings per artist per day, which they'd sell for about $25 apiece. It is estimated that between 1955 and the 1980s, they created more than 200,000 paintings. Carroll called herself "Queen of the Road" for her role in the Florida Highwaymen. The only woman in a group that was overwhelmingly male, her paintings had a practical purpose: They kept her seven children fed and clothed. She served as the first president of the Florida Highwaymen Artist and History Center, Inc., and presented one of her paintings to Michelle Obama when she visited the White House in 2011 for the White House First Lady's Luncheon. On Sundays, Carroll could be found singing and preaching in her ministry. She first picked up a brush in 1957 when she met Harold Newton, who helped her learn how to paint. She took pride in keeping her Buick pristine as she traveled the state, selling her paintings on roadsides and at restaurants and hotels that wouldn't serve her because of Jim Crow laws.

In the mid-1990s, the *St. Petersburg Times* ran a couple of newspaper articles and called the group the Florida Highwaymen for the first time. The name stuck, and the articles sparked an interest in their work, which began to sell for higher prices. Nowadays their paintings are valued at thousands of dollars each and are exhibited in galleries like the Museum of Florida History and the National Museum of African American History and Culture.

For many years, reading and writing was not expected of Black people—in fact, for many enslaved Black people, it was against the law to learn to read and write. As a result, there weren't many Black-centered books with Black characters, and only rarely any Black characters in children's books. When Black characters did appear in mainstream publications, they were usually stereotypical images of Sambo-like characters with big lips and other exaggerated features that reinforced stereotypes about Black people.

Black cartoonists have had to deal with a lot of racism within the cartoon industry. During the Golden Age of Comics, which lasted from the 1930s through the 1950s, few Black cartoonists were recognized for their talent because they were only being published in Black press outlets like the Chicago Defender. In 1947, All-Negro Comics became the first comic book company with an all-Black staff. The first issue of the magazine they created was a stunning success, but they never printed a second edition because white paper mill owners refused to sell them paper to print the issue.

It wasn't until 1970 that the Coretta Scott King Awards were created to reward Black illustrators and writers for creating children's books for Black readers. As the demand for Black illustrators to fill the pages of books grew, so did the opportunities. Now there are many Black illustrators who create images, cartoons, and other artwork for books, comics, and graphic novels.

JACKIE ORMES:
First Black Professional Cartoonist

Jackie Ormes is widely considered to be the first professional Black cartoonist in America. She created four comic strips: *Torchy Brown in Dixie to Harlem* (1937), *Candy* (1945), *Patty Jo 'n' Ginger* (1946), and *Torchy Brown, Heartbeats* (1950). After high school, Ormes went to work at her first job as a proofreader for the *Pittsburgh Courier*. Eventually, she began contributing further by writing news stories at the paper and eventually began to draw comics for them. In 1945, she went to work for the *Chicago Defender* as a comics artist and contributing journalist. Her 1946 debut of the comic strip *Patty Jo 'n' Ginger* was so well received that a doll was created from the character Patty Jo, the first Black doll created from a comic strip.

D Is for Doll-Making

In the United States, for many years, it was difficult to find any Black dolls. When they were available, they were usually dolls with stereotypically features echoing the stereotypes of a "mammy" or "sambo." These dolls were usually played with by white children, and it was difficult to find realistic Black dolls in toy stores. In 1911, when Richard Henry Boyd could not find accurately representational Black dolls for his children, he founded the Negro Doll Company. Mattel introduced its first Black Barbie doll in 1967, but the doll, which they named Francine, had white features and straight hair. In 2012, the National Black Doll Museum of History and Culture opened in Mansfield, Massachusetts. Its collection includes over 6,000 Black dolls and action figures. However, doll making companies that cater to Black children are becoming more prevalent. Trinity Designs is a Texas-based doll manufacturer that creates sorority girl-themed dolls as well as dolls for adults. Columbus, Ohio-based Uzuri Kid Kidz has been making Black dolls since 1997. In Nigeria, "Queens of Africa" dolls are outselling Barbie. These dolls have authentically Black features, natural hair, and wear traditional clothing made of African cloth.

Elenora "Rukiya" Brown is an American doll maker. She grew up in Chicago in the 1960s and began making dolls to relieve stress and express herself artistically. As a child, the only dolls she could find in stores were white, so she began making dolls for friends and family members out of things she found in the park across the street from her home, such as corn husks. She moved to New Orleans as a teenager and later studied textiles in England. In 1994, she returned from England to New Orleans and began making dolls. She was discovered by a gallery owner at the New Orleans Jazz Festival who recognized her talent and helped her find opportunities to exhibit her collections of dolls. In 2005, Rukiya was forced to return to Chicago after Hurricane Katrina displaced her family. She is now back in New Orleans but debuts her collections in Chicago to give thanks for the hospitality the city showed the people displaced by the hurricane. Rukiya continues to make and sell her soft sculptured dolls, which celebrate her African heritage and the history of African people. Each doll is one of a kind.

NICOLE MILLER:
Video Artistry

Nicole Miller is a video artist who uses film and installations to explore issues of prejudice and the reality of Black life in America. She has exhibited her work in Geneva, Switzerland, at Kunst-Werke in Berlin, Germany, at LAXART in Los Angeles, California, and at the Dallas Contemporary Art Museum in Dallas, Texas, among other places. She is well-known for her work *The Conductor*, which is a silent film featuring a Black man in a Jimi Hendrix T-shirt conducting an imaginary symphony. The film is reminiscent of historic silent films and animations because of the main character's bold gestures. Miller's work speaks to issues of race and racial history.

CAMILLE BILLOPS:
Filmmaker of the Black Diaspora

For most of the early twentieth century, Black filmmakers had to work outside of the white Hollywood mainstream. When Black characters were depicted in white films, they were often in blackface and portrayed stereotypically either as bumbling fools or villains. The earliest Black filmmakers worked in the 1920s and 1930s creating films that are now called "race films." There were about 500 short films and feature-length films made by Black filmmakers such as Tressie Souders, who became the first known African American woman to direct a feature film with *A Woman's Error* (1922), and Maria Williams, credited as the first Black female film producer for the silent crime drama *The Flames of Wrath* (1923). Their films were made primarily for Black audiences and defied the stereotypes in white films of the time. In Black-made films, the characters were all well-rounded and could be heroic. Hollywood has recently seen an increase in the number of Black women filmmakers like Ava DuVernay, Nia DaCosta, Nikyatu Jusu, and Janicza Bravo, as well as many others. However, there are still complaints that not as many Black filmmakers get credit for their creations, especially every year at the Academy Awards.

Camille Billops, an internationally recognized sculptor, painter, and filmmaker, was born in Los Angeles in 1933. Her appearance was unique: Journalist Amena Meer says she had beads in her braids, feathers, a man's hat on, and black-rimmed eyes; her upper lip was hairy, and she wore Afro-Asian necklaces.

Billops traces the genesis of her art back to her parents' love of cooking and dressmaking. Despite beginning her career as a sculptor, ceramicist, and painter, Billops is best known as a filmmaker of the Black diaspora. Her parents were always making home movies of their daughters, Billie and Camille, accustoming Billops to a life both in front of the camera and behind it; her signature films are as intimate as family home movies. Several of Billops's films have been collaborations with and stories about members of her family. They were coproduced with her husband James Hatch and by their production company, Mom and Pop Productions; Hatch's son was director of photography.

Billops made *Suzanne, Suzanne*, a film about her niece Suzanne's recovery from heroin addiction. The film dissects the relationship between Billie, Billops's sister, and her sister's daughter Suzanne, both of whom were abused by her sister's husband. Five more films followed, including *Finding Christa* in 1991, a highly autobiographical documentary that won a Grand Jury Prize at the 1992 Sundance Film Festival. Billops giving up her very young daughter and their reunion twenty years later were documented in *Finding Christa*. While society judged Billops harshly and urged her to repent, Billops remained unapologetic about giving her daughter up for adoption. Billops had been told by her own mother that motherhood is an essential component of womanhood. She wasn't happy with this and by age ten had decided she didn't want children. For her, Black women's lives were endurance contests, struggles to survive abusive or alcoholic men, and their children were part of the yoke that hindered their freedom.

Rather than allowing her family to adopt the child, Billops drove the four-year-old to Los Angeles Children's Home Society, an orphanage. She drove away in her black Volkswagen Beetle after asking Christa to go inside to the bathroom. Some family members were upset by the decision, while others forgave Ms. Billops. According to Carol Penn, a cousin, "It's easy to label this brilliant woman a demon. But she was complex and conflicted, and she did it out of love; she just didn't feel herself capable of being a mother." Later, Christa was adopted by a jazz singer in Oakland. Billops often told people that she regretted not giving her daughter up for adoption sooner, when Christa was still young and could have forgotten her. Christa, however, held a strong psychological grip on her mother. Even as Billops struggled with dementia, she could not escape her grief for her daughter. She frequently thought about Christa. It always came back to Christa, no matter what she talked about.

After twenty years, Billops heard from Christa, now a vocalist, pianist, and composer who went by Christa Victoria. She sent Billops a cassette of a song she wrote and asked to see her. Initially, Billops was doubtful. Having compartmentalized her guilt, she thought that part of her life was long behind her. The documentary concludes with Christa Victoria, an artistic and vibrant young woman, being allowed back into the life of her birth mother. Nevertheless, the story doesn't end there. Off camera, the mother and daughter, both possessed a diva temperament, had a troubled relationship entangled in guilt and fueled by competitiveness. The jealous and spiteful Billops told *Topic* magazine that Christa was trying to claim credit for the movie, while Christa still sought to understand why her mother had given her up.

Christa was rejected a second time by Billops after the reunion when she barred Christa from attending the

Sundance Awards. Although her daughter begged, Billops shut out any communication, leaving the real-life story to end sadly for both. During an interview, Dion Hatch, the stepson of Ms. Billops, said they were very much alike, two very strong-willed people. According to Mr. Hatch, Christa was always seeking an explanation for why she had been given up, and Billops was afraid to deal with that. Ms. Billops would not let anyone mention Christa's name, he said, "but then she would spend hours talking about Christa herself."

Christa died of heart failure at the age of fifty-nine in 2016 as a result of her refusal to undergo a necessary operation; she was found alone in her Bronx apartment. Christa wrote her mother another letter a few days before she died. In this letter, she apologized for any harm she may have caused.

Other movie credits for Billops include *Older Women and Love* in 1987 (inspired by her aunt's love affair), *The KKK Boutique*

Ain't Just Rednecks (1994), *Take Your Bags* (1998), and *A String of Pearls* (2002).

Billops once said, "I don't know if I am that conscious of it, but some people say that our films have a tendency toward dirty laundry. The films say it like it is, rather than how people want it to be. Maybe it is my character that tends to want to do that, because I think the visual [artist] in me wants to say the same kind of thing. So, I don't know if I consciously did it; I think it is just my own spirit."

ELIZABETH CATLETT:
Female and Black

Elizabeth Catlett, born in 1915, was an African American sculptor and graphic artist best known for her depictions of African American women in the twentieth century. Catlett acknowledged that her art influenced young Black women. It had previously been nearly unthinkable to be a Black woman sculptor. There were only a few of them, and they all had very tough circumstances to overcome. "But," Catlett said, "you can be a Black woman sculptor, a printmaker, a teacher, a mother, a grandmother, and keep a house. It takes commitment, but you can do it. All you have to do is decide."

Her mother and father were both the children of freed slaves. Her grandmother told her stories about the capture of their people in Africa and the hardships of plantation life. Because of her dedication to African American issues and experiences, her work can be described as social realism. It is the artist's intent to convey social messages through her works rather than pure aesthetics. Art students studying race, gender, and class issues learn from her work, which focused on social injustice, the human condition, historical figures, women, and the relationship between mother and child. These topics were directly related to the African American experience in the twentieth century, and her art also drew on some influences from Mexican culture and narratives.

From sensitive images of mothers to confrontational symbols of Black Power, to her portraits of women such as Maria Shriver, Harriet Tubman, and Rosa Parks, she believed that art can play a part in defining transnational and ethnic identities. In her best-known works, Black women are portrayed as strong and maternal. Voluptuous women with broad hips and shoulders display confidence and power, often with their torsos thrust forward to signal attitude. Their faces are mask-like and tend to be upturned. Catlett's "The Negro Woman," a series of fifteen linoleum cuts from 1946–1947, emphasizes the issues of discrimination and racism faced by African American women during this time. As well as depicting the strength and courage of these women, this series highlighted the contributions of historically prominent African American women including Harriet Tubman and Phillis Wheatley.

Catlett said, "I have always wanted my art to [be of] service [to] my people—to reflect us, to relate to us, to stimulate us, to make us aware of our potential." She was a feminist and a civil rights activist before these modern movements took shape, pursuing a career in art despite segregation and the lack of female role models. "I don't think art can change things," Catlett said. "I think writing can do more. But art can prepare people for change, it can be educational and persuasive in people's thinking."

> **"Art for me must develop from a necessity within my people. It must answer a question, or wake somebody up, or give a shove in the right direction—our liberation."**
>
> **—Elizabeth Catlett,**
> sculptor and graphic artist whose work often focused on the female experience

FAITH RINGGOLD:
Immersive and Radical Power

Faith Ringgold, born in Harlem, New York in 1930, is an American painter, writer, mixed-media sculptor, and performance artist best known for her narrative quilts. With a career combining the multidisciplinary practices of the Harlem Renaissance with the political art of young Black artists today, she is one of the most influential cultural figures of her generation.

During the 1950s, Ringgold's mother was a popular Harlem clothing designer and seamstress, while her father was an avid storyteller. Her parents raised her in an environment that fostered creativity. In the wake of the Harlem Renaissance, Ringgold's childhood home in Harlem was surrounded by a vibrant arts scene; Duke Ellington and Langston Hughes lived in the same neighborhood, and her childhood friend Sonny Rollins, who grew up to become a prominent jazz musician, played saxophone at her family's parties. Ringgold experimented with crayons as a young girl rather than more active pursuits because of her chronic asthma,. Her mother, Willi Posey, encouraged her artistic interests. She also taught her how to sew and use fabric creatively, and how to quilt in the African American tradition. Young Faith also learned quilting from her grandmother, who had learned it from her slave mother, Susie Shannon.

The people, poetry, and music that Ringgold experienced as a child, as well as the racism, sexism, and segregation that she dealt with in her daily life, all greatly affected the development of her artwork. To get away from painting, which felt locked within Western/European traditions, Ringgold chose to work with fabric. Her use of quilts facilitated her advocacy on behalf of the feminist movement, as she was able to roll up her quilts to carry them to the gallery without requiring any assistance.

Since no publishers were interested in publishing her autobiography at the time, Ringgold quilted her stories for people to hear; her work was both autobiographical and artistic. She stated in an interview with the Crocker

Art Museum, "In 1983, I began writing stories on my quilts as an alternative. This way, when my quilts are displayed or photographed, people can still read my stories." Her first quilt story is entitled "Who's Afraid of Aunt Jemima?" (1983); it depicts the story of Aunt Jemima as a matriarch restaurateur and fictionally revises "the most maligned Black female stereotype." In "Change: Faith Ringgold's Over 100 Pounds Weight Loss Performance Story Quilt" (1986), she tackles the topic of a woman who struggles with cultural beauty norms, a woman whose intelligence and political sensitivity allow her to see the inherent contradictions in her position, and who finds the inspiration to turn the entire challenge into art.

Story quilts from Ringgold's French Collection tell the stories of historical African American women who changed the world (as in "The Sunflowers Quilting Bee at Arles"). The quilts also call out and redirect the male gaze; they demonstrate the immersive power of historical fantasy and childlike imagination. Many of her quilts went on to inspire the children's books that she later made, such as *Dinner at Aunt Connie's House* (1993) published by Hyperion Books, based on "The Dinner Quilt" (1988).

She explores gender and racial identities in her story quilts, which are richly made with diverse textures. Ringgold's fabric pieces are among the most important artworks of the past fifty years, combining local traditions with global references to tell the story of our nation. As an artist and mother, Ringgold has documented her own life as well as amplifying the struggles for social justice and equity over the last six decades. Through her experimental story quilts,

Faith Ringgold has produced a body of work that bears witness to the complexity of the American experience, including some of the most indelible artworks concerning the Civil Rights Era.

———————

Another quilter of note is **Sherry Shine**. She has always loved drawing; at the age of three, she created her first mural (a large drawing of her whole family and some neighbors) on her bedroom wall. After she painted the mural, she then tried to hide it behind pillows. That got her into trouble. As a teenager, Shine was mentored by an art teacher who nurtured her talent. Shine attended Morris Brown College in Atlanta, Georgia, on a scholarship, majoring in business and hotel management. Many years after graduating, Shine again became interested in art and took some general classes at the Fashion Institute of Technology. When a friend who made quilts using a long arm quilting machine offered to teach Shine how to quilt, she was hooked!

Shine learned how to cut and piece fabrics together using traditional quilting techniques. To understand what she needed to do, Shine attended a lecture on dyeing fabrics and how to make an art quilt. "My creativity and curiosity were ignited, and my passion for art quilts was formed," recalls Shine. Her art has been shown across the country in galleries, colleges, and museums including at Bank Street College in New York, the Michigan State University Museum in East Lansing, the Bedford Brooklyn Public Library and Manhattan Community College in New York City, and the National Constitutional Center in Philadelphia. Shine lives with her family in New Jersey.

The world of contemporary Black women's art is exciting and fresh. Black female artists use their creations to explore all the issues facing Black women today, and they do it with gusto, in bold and surprising ways. When you have an opportunity to explore Black women's art, it will open your eyes and reinvigorate your senses. Black women's art is where it's at. Get yourself to a museum and explore it when you have a chance.

chapter five

BEYOND THE CATWALK & THE STAGE

BLACK DANCERS AND MODELS

There is barely any history of Black ballet dancers in the American ballet world because Black dancers were neither invited nor allowed to perform in American ballet companies for many years. This exclusion persisted on account of racial bias and because the ballet world upheld an unrealistic body type of very thin dancers as its ideal. The ballet world began to change its body type ideal at the end of the twentieth century and has since begun to embrace Black ballet dancers.

When Arthur Mitchell founded the Dance Theatre of Harlem, which relied on Black dancers, opportunities began to arise for other Black ballerinas to join the dance world, including **Ingrid Silva**, who was invited to dance with the company. The Dance Theatre of Harlem was founded with the intention of elevating dancers of all colors in the world of ballet performance. Beginning with just thirty students, it attracted nearly 400 students within months of its opening and has continued to attract talented Black dancers since its founding in 1969, at the height of the Civil Rights Movement.

INGRID SILVA:
When They Don't Make Shoes for You

Ingrid Silva, an internationally noted ballet dancer, was born in 1988 in Rio de Janeiro, Brazil. Her father served in the air force and her mother was a maid. She began dancing at age eight through a community outreach program, and went on to train at Dançando Para Não Dançar in Brazil. She moved to New York City at age eighteen because there were few opportunities for her to dance in Brazil; there, she met the founder of the Dance Theatre of Harlem, Arthur Mitchell, who invited her to dance with the theatre. Silva has called for greater diversity in ballet, explaining that she had to color her pointe shoes brown because they were only made for white skin tones. Outside of ballet, she is a cofounder of EmpowerHerNY, a social media platform that allows different women to take over its Instagram account. She said, "[By] being a Black ballerina, I am breaking through barriers."

PRINCE// MHOON COOPER:
Black Girl Change-Maker

Princess Mhoon Cooper, a Chicago native, is a choreographer, producer, educator, and scholar. She received her training at the Alyo Children's Dance Theatre, the Joseph Holmes Dance Studio, and the Muntu Dance Theatre of Chicago, and also studied at Howard University, earning both a Bachelor of Fine Arts degree in dance and a master's degree in public history. Her research is on dance history and the Black experience in dance. In 2015, she was recognized by *Huffington Post* as one of twenty-six choreographers you should know. *Dance Magazine* also named her to their list of the top twenty-five dance choreographers in the world to watch as part of the

Women's Choreography Project presentation called "This Woman's Work." In 2016, First Lady Michelle Obama invited Cooper to the White House for a celebration of Black women in dance. She has also worked with the White House Initiative on Educational Excellence for African Americans and was named by the Obama administration as a Black Girl Change Maker. In 2015, Cooper also won the Helen Hayes Award for Best Choreography in a Musical. She was one of thirty-seven artists who was invited to Zambia for the 2015 Barefeet Theatre Festival, an event sponsored by UNICEF. She founded the Princess Mhoon Dance Institute in Washington, DC, and is its chief choreographer and director. Cooper teaches at American University in Washington, DC. She works as a guest director and choreographer on various national stage productions.

ANNE RAVEN WILKIN/ON:
Principal Dancer

Although **Anne Raven Wilkinson** was fair-skinned, she grew up on 150th Street in Harlem (above what she called "the Mason-Dixon Line of New York [City]"). She and her mother were often questioned by strangers when they traveled to other parts of the city because the two of them didn't match others' preconceptions about how African Americans were supposed to look, dress, or speak. When these curious and confounded strangers asked

Wilkinson's mother, "What *are* you?" she would reply, "We're Americans."

An uncle gifted young Anne ballet lessons at Swoboda School, later known as the Ballet Russe School, for her ninth birthday. While Wilkinson had a light complexion, her race still made it difficult for her to gain entry to a ballet company. Wilkinson auditioned for a full-time position with the troupe in 1954. While her talent was recognized, she was rejected. Wilkinson's friend told her after several auditions for the Ballet Lopotre, "Raven, they can't afford [to accept] you because of your race." Her fellow ballet students told her to stay out of the contest, but she was unstoppable, and eventually it paid off! In 1955, Wilkinson finally broke the color barrier when she began dancing full-time with the Ballet Russe of Monte Carlo.

During Wilkinson's six years with the Ballet Russe, she experienced both happiness and hardship. She was promoted to the position of soloist in her second season and performed several leading roles, such as dancing the waltz solo in *Les Sylphides*. As an African American touring with a dance company, she encountered many obstacles, particularly in segregated areas of the South. Wilkinson kept her race secret when the troupe stayed in "whites only" hotels. Some of the other dancers urged Wilkinson to claim that she was Spanish because of her fair complexion; but even though she often used makeup to lighten her skin for performances, she did not hide who she was if directly asked. As much as she didn't want to put the company at risk, she also didn't want to deny the truth. She felt she could not say, "I'm not Black" if someone asked her directly.

Things went well during the first two years. There were many foreign dancers in the company, including several South Americans, so her race was not an issue. However, in 1957, when a hotel owner in Atlanta, Georgia, asked her outright if she was Black, Wilkinson refused to lie and was barred from staying with the troupe. She was taken to a "colored" motel in a "colored" taxi. Later on the same tour, two Ku Klux Klan members bolted onto the stage to interrupt a performance in Montgomery, Alabama, asking, "Where's the nigra?" The men left when none of the company members responded to them. In fact, whenever it looked like there would be trouble after a performance, Wilkinson's colleagues would appear at the stage door to escort her. She continued to perform soloist roles wherever the company toured.

But Wilkinson's racial identity eventually became more widely known, and discrimination became a larger problem in both her personal and professional life. As a result of years of discrimination, Wilkinson left the Ballet Russe touring ensemble in 1961. Although she then auditioned for several American ballet companies, including the New York City Ballet, American Ballet Theatre, and the Metropolitan Opera Ballet, she was not accepted. Devastated, she gave up dancing for two years.

She joined the Dutch National Ballet as a second soloist in the mid-1960s. Wilkinson moved to the Netherlands in 1967 and stayed with the troupe for seven years before retiring and moving back to New York at the age of thirty-eight. Wilkinson performed with the New York City Opera until 1985. When she turned fifty, she stopped dancing, but continued on as an actress until 2011, when the company folded.

During her later years, Wilkinson formed a special friendship with Misty Copeland. Wilkinson's story was also brought back into the public eye by Copeland's breakout success: Wilkinson was featured in the 2016 documentary *Black Ballerina*, and a book based on Wilkinson's life titled *Trailblazer: The Story of Ballerina Raven Wilkinson* was published with a foreword written by Copeland. In June 2015, Wilkinson received the 2015 Dance/USA Trustee Award.

Black Ballerinas

Debra Austin was the first Black American woman to become a principal dancer for a major American ballet company when she joined the Pennsylvania Ballet. She was also the first Black female principal dancer in the New York City Ballet.

Katherine Dunham, who created the Dunham Technique, is heralded as the "Matriarch of Black Dance." **Pearl Primus** famously documented and preserved African dance as an anthropologist and dancer-choreographer. **Lula Washington** established a world-class dance company and dance academy in inner-city Los Angeles.

From ballet to modern dance and from Lindy Hop to hip-hop, countless Black women revolutionized dance, leaving an indelible mark. They have formed companies, written books, created choreography, taught the next generation of legends, and wowed audiences near and far with their inspired works and performances. Movement inspired them to rise above poverty, racism, and even ageism. Here are some other beautiful and graceful Black women who have achieved their dancing dreams and should be known and celebrated:

- In addition to her numerous leading roles as a member of the New York City Ballet's corps de ballet, **Aesha Ash** has danced as a soloist with the Béjart Ballet, Alonzo King's LINES Ballet, and Morphoses/The Wheeldon Company. Her appointment at the School of American Ballet marked the first time an African American woman became a permanent faculty member at that institution. In 2011, after retiring from performing, she founded the Swan Dreams Project to dispel stereotypes about Black women in ballet. The initiative advocates for and inspires African American communities, and in particular young ballet dancers whose opportunities may be limited because of their race or socioeconomic status. "I want to help change the demoralized, objectified, and caricatured images of African American women by showing the world that beauty is not reserved for any particular race or socioeconomic background," Ash says on her website. In addition to exposing African American communities to ballet, she hopes to increase their involvement with and patronage of this beautiful art form. Ash wants Black youth to know that they are not limited by stereotypes nor by their environment.

- **Lauren Anderson** (born 1965) was a principal dancer with the Houston Ballet. Having been told as a young adult that her body was too muscular for ballet and that she would be better suited to musical theater, Anderson adopted a meatless diet to slim down and began taking Pilates classes to lengthen her muscles. Her sacrifices paid off. It was a historic milestone in American ballet when she emerged as the first Black principal dancer for a major company in 1990. She was also one of the few Black ballerinas ever to take the helm of a major ballet company anywhere in the world. Her ballet roles included *Don Quixote*, *Cleopatra*, and *The Nutcracker*. After retiring from the Houston Ballet in 2006, she retired completely from the dance industry in 2009. Anderson revealed that she had been an alcoholic until July 2009. After being pulled over for speeding, she soon found herself in county jail. Anderson was given a wake-up call by the judge after winding up in court. Since then, Anderson has been living sober and attends Alcoholics Anonymous meetings every day, no matter where she is. In the spring of 2016, the Smithsonian's National

Museum of African American History and Culture recognized her with a permanent exhibit on her groundbreaking life. She was recently inducted into the Texas Women's Hall of Fame.

PEARL PRIMUS:
Child Returned Home

Dr. Pearl Primus was a dancer, choreographer, teacher, and anthropologist who studied traditional African and Caribbean dance and created performance pieces that stunned audiences with their athleticism and social commentary. To the amazement of her audiences, she could leap five feet in the air.

Born in 1919 in Port of Spain, Trinidad, Primus immigrated to the United States when she was two years old with her parents, who settled in New York City. She initially studied biology with the goal of becoming a medical doctor, but once she finished her bachelor's degree and sought work at a medical lab, she discovered that she was shut out of any job in the medical field due to her race. Instead, she took on a series of odd jobs and found work with the dance unit of the National Youth Administration, where she discovered a natural talent for movement and dance. She went on to receive a scholarship from the New Dance Group and studied modern dance with them. In 1944, she debuted her first solo choreographic work, "African Ceremonial," which featured material drawn from her early studies of Black culture and heritage.

Primus often based her dances on the situational elements of racial issues as well as on the work of Black writers. In 1944, she interpreted Langston Hughes's poem "The Negro Speaks of Rivers," followed in 1945 by "Strange Fruit," based on the poignant poem about lynchings by Abel Meeropol (known by his pen name of Lewis Allan), which had famously been recorded as a song by Billie Holiday. Primus received a Rosenwald Foundation grant to study dance in West Africa in 1948; while there, she immersed herself in research and was given special access, allowing her to study dance movements that were reserved solely for men. She was formally adopted by the King of Ife, H.E. Sir Adesoji Aderemi II, who ruled as the spiritual leader of the Yoruba in Nigeria. He renamed her Omowale, which translates to "child returned home."

Back in the United States, Primus used her studies in Africa to inform her work. Notably, she choreographed her dance piece "The Wedding," which relied on African dance movements. She opened her own dance company, which grew into the Pearl Primus Dance Language Institute, known for its blending of ballet and modern dance styles with traditional African, African American, and Caribbean movements. Visiting the American South, Primus embedded herself with sharecroppers, even being hiring on as one and working in the fields herself. She also returned to Trinidad, the country of her birth, to study its dance traditions. She earned an MA and a PhD from New York University and later continued her academic work in ethnic studies at the Five Colleges consortium in Massachusetts.

Dr. Primus was honored with the "Star of Africa" medal for distinguished service in the arts by the Liberian Government in 1949, and she was awarded the National Medal of Arts in 1991 by President George Herbert Walker Bush, among other awards. Pearl Primus died of diabetes in 1994 following a remarkable life.

LULA WASHINGTON:
Reflecting Black History and Culture

Lula Washington is an artistic director, choreographer, teacher, and dancer who established a top-notch dance company and academy in inner-city Los Angeles. Her family was too poor for her to take dance lessons; she worked nights in hamburger stands, skating rinks, and movie theaters so she could afford to buy clothes for school. It wasn't until she was a nursing student at Harbor Community College in Los Angeles that she experienced modern dance. A teacher took Washington and other students to see the Alvin Ailey American Dance Theater at UCLA. She was so mesmerized by the beauty of Ailey's dancers that she decided to pursue dance as a career. The school told her that at twenty-two, she was too old to begin a dance career, and she was turned down by UCLA's dance program. But her appeal was successful, and Washington was admitted to UCLA.

Lula Washington established the Los Angeles Contemporary Dance Company after graduating, later changing its name to the Lula Washington Dance Theatre. Washington has earned national and international respect as a dance leader, teacher, entrepreneur, and choreographer since establishing the dance company. She blends African and modern dance, ballet, and performance art in her choreography. Numerous honors have been bestowed upon her, including a choreography fellowship from the National Endowment for the Arts and the California Dance Educators Award of Excellence. Washington's dances are often inspired by the African American experience as well as current global events and local events in the Los Angeles area. Her work explores topics such as being houseless, 9/11, police brutality, the Civil Rights Movement, and the Underground Railroad. Washington has also choreographed for movies including *Avatar* and *The Little Mermaid*. She has composed classical works to Bach and Vivaldi, as well as African dance and hip-hop pieces.

Black women dare to thrive, even when they are isolated within the spaces they occupy. They dance and create, even when they lack support and encouragement. Here are a few other dancers and choreographers of note:

- Dancer and choreographer **Judith Ann Jamison** is the artistic director emerita of Alvin Ailey American Dance Theater.

- **Ebony Williams** has rapidly established herself as Hollywood's go-to choreographer. Born and raised in Boston, Massachusetts, she discovered her passion for dance at the age of eight, doing hip-hop dance moves with other kids in the neighborhood before going on to study jazz and tap at the Roxbury Center for the Performing Arts.

- Singer, songwriter, dancer, and actress **Mya Marie Harrison** is known by her stage name Mýa. Born into a musical family, she studied ballet, jazz, and tap dance as a child. Today, she's a Grammy Award-winning artist.

- As *The New York Times* notes, **Fatima Robinson** is "one of the most sought-after hip-hop and popular music choreographers in the world."

MISTY COPELAND:
Taking Center Stage

Misty Copeland is the first African American woman to become a principal dancer for the American Ballet Theatre, one of the largest ballet companies in the United States. She began learning ballet when she was thirteen, which is usually considered a bit late to start. Her family's financial situation made it difficult for her to begin her dance studies, but once she started, it was only a few months before she moved up to dancing en pointe and rapidly became a young prodigy. She played a leading role in *The Nutcracker* just eight months after starting ballet and was performing on a professional level shortly after that. This was unheard of amongst classical dancers, since many ballerinas spend their whole lives training to reach that point. She drew lots of media attention and quickly became a prominent figure in ballet.

At fifteen, she won first place at the Music Center Spotlight Awards. She studied dance at the San Francisco Ballet School and at American Ballet Theatre's Summer Intensive. In 2000, she was declared the American Ballet Theater's Coca-Cola Scholar. She joined the American Ballet Theater in 2000; in 2015, she was promoted to principal dancer, making her the first Black ballerina in the company's history to be named a principal dancer. Copeland has been featured on many television shows, such as *60 Minutes*, *CBS Sunday Morning*, *The Today Show*, and *This Week with George Stephanopoulos*. She has also been featured in magazines including *Vogue*, *Essence*, *Ebony*, and *People*. In 2014, President Barack Obama appointed Copeland to the President's Council on Fitness, Sports, and Nutrition. Copeland has written two books, a *New York Times* bestselling memoir entitled *Life in Motion*, and a picture book called *Firebird*. "I knew that I just didn't have it in me to give up," she said, "even if I sometimes felt like a fool for continuing to believe."

> **"The path to your success is not as fixed and inflexible as you think."**
>
> **—Misty Copeland,**
>
> American ballet dancer; she started ballet at the age of thirteen and made history as the first African American female principal dancer with the American Ballet Theatre

JANET COLLINS:
Unapologetically Black

Janet Collins was a ballet dancer, choreographer, and teacher. She was born in New Orleans, Louisiana, in 1917, and moved with her family to Los Angeles when she was four years old. In Los Angeles, Collins received her first dance training at a community center; there were few ballet instructors who would accept Black students at the time. She gained skill in dance, and by the age of sixteen, she was ready to audition for the prestigious Ballet Russe de Monte Carlo. She was accepted into the dance troupe, but declined their offer when they told her she would be required to whiten her skin and face in order to perform with them. Instead, she joined the Dunham Company and began to dance in New York City. In 1948, she danced in her own choreography on a shared program at the 92 Street YMHA. The next year,

Collins began to dance on Broadway and went on to receive the Donaldson Award for the best dancer on Broadway for her work in Cole Porter's *Out of This World*. She became the first Black ballerina to perform at the Metropolitan Opera in 1951 and continued to perform with them until 1955. In later life, she taught modern dance at Balanchine's School of American Ballet in New York City, and also at Marymount Manhattan College from 1951 until 1972. In 1974, she retired and joined a religious order. Collins performed and had a breakthrough career despite the prevalence of harsh racial barriers for Black ballet dancers during her life. When her company toured the South, an understudy often had to take over her roles due to rules that prohibited her from dancing on stage. In 1974, the Alvin Ailey American Dance Theater paid homage to her as a notable woman in dance.

If Black ballet dancers had it rough, so too did Black models. Not only did the Black aesthetic not fit in with the world of fashion photography, the camera film itself wasn't even engineered correctly to capture the subtleties of Black skin in photographs. These next few models dared to defy the stereotypical norms of fashion photography and broke barriers when it came to modeling.

Black Is Beautiful

Donyale Luna was the first Black supermodel as well as an actress. She appeared on the cover of *British Vogue* in 1966, long before Black supermodels were receiving mainstream coverage. Luna was born in 1945. In 1963, when she was still in high school, she was spotted by photographer David McCabe, who was stunned by her slender figure and prominent bone structure. He invited her to move to New York immediately. She took a year to decide to make that move, but soon took the fashion world by storm. Within a few months of her arrival, she was under contract to work with Richard Avedon, Bob Dylan, and Jean Shrimpton. Newspapers across the country declared her the first Black supermodel. Luna's entry into the New York fashion scene occurred just a few months after the Civil Rights Bill passed, which banned discrimination in hiring practices and segregation in public places; however, she still faced plenty of discrimination. In 1965, an artist drew sketches of her for the cover of *Harper's Bazaar*. The magazine received complaints about the resulting image and even lost subscribers. This racial discrimination led Luna to move to London, where she continued modeling. She was a muse for the artist Salvador Dalí, who based some of his artwork on her. She was also an actress, appearing in the movie *Blow-Up* in 1966. In 1969, she landed a role in Federico Fellini's *Satyricon* and later appeared in Carmelo Bene's *Salomé*. Luna died of a drug overdose in 1979.

Naomi Ruth Sims is widely considered to be one of the first Black supermodels to achieve prominence. She was the first Black model to appear on the cover of *Ladies Home Journal*, then one of the foremost American women's magazines, in 1968. Sims was born in Oxford, Mississippi, in 1948; her parents divorced soon after she was born. Her mother moved the family to Pittsburgh, Pennsylvania. Due to illness, her mother was forced to put young Naomi and her two sisters into foster care. In high school, the 5'10" Sims was teased because of her height; but she managed to qualify for a scholarship to study at the Fashion Institute of Technology in New York. She also took night classes in psychology at New York University. Sims had a hard time breaking into modeling; at first, she tried to find employment by applying to the modeling agencies in New York, but she was told that her skin was too dark. Sims decided to approach the fashion photographers directly and had a breakthrough when Gösta Peterson agreed to photograph her for *The New York Times* fashion supplement in August 1967. Despite *The New York Times* coverage, Sims still found it difficult to find work. She went to Wilhemina Cooper, a former model who was opening her own agency, and asked her to take her on as one of her models. Cooper agreed, and Sims was selected to appear in a nationwide TV advertising campaign for AT&T. After that, her career took off. She became the first Black supermodel to appear on the cover of *Life* magazine in 1969, and she was widely sought after for work by many of the most popular magazines of the day. Sims retired from modeling in 1973; she opened her own business selling textured wigs, which eventually grew into a multimillion-dollar enterprise. She also authored several books, including *All About Health and Beauty for the Black Woman*, *How to Be a Top Model*, and *All About Success for the Black Woman*, as well as an advice column for teenage girls in *Right On!* magazine.

Beverly Johnson is an actress, singer, model, and businesswoman. She was the first Black model to appear on the cover of American *Vogue* in 1974. She was born in Buffalo, New York, in 1952. In high school, Johnson was a competitive swimmer and was also interested in the Civil Rights Movement. In order to make changes in society, she aspired to be a lawyer and started classes at Northeastern University in Boston. On summer break in 1971, she decided to try modeling to earn some money. She quickly landed a contract with *Glamour* magazine; over the course of her career, she went on to grace the covers of more than 500 magazines and journals. But her journey to the top was not without its struggles. Johnson knew she wanted to appear on the cover of *Vogue*, launch a cosmetics line, and write a book, but was told by legendary agent Eileen Ford that she'd never get a *Vogue* cover. Undeterred, Johnson switched agencies and signed with Wilhelmina Cooper. When she finally got the cover shot, she refused to be pigeonholed as a Black model, saying, "I'm the biggest model, period." In addition to her modeling, Johnson is also a singer, actress, and writer and has penned two books, *Beverly Johnson's Guide to a Life of Health and Beauty* and *True Beauty: Secrets of Radiant Beauty for Women of Every Age and Color*. She has appeared on television in the series *Martin*, *Law & Order*, *Lois & Clark: The New Adventures of Superman*, *The Parent 'Hood*, and *3rd Rock from the Sun*. She is also a successful businesswoman and the founder, chairwoman, and CEO of Beverly Johnson Enterprises, LLC, a luxurious lifestyle brand.

MAR/HA P. JOHN/ON:
Stonewall Liberator

Marsha P. Johnson was a gay liberation and AIDS activist and drag performer. She was born in 1945 in Elizabeth, New Jersey, one of seven siblings who were raised in the Mount Teman African Methodist Episcopal Church. In 1966, she left Elizabeth for New York City and transformed herself into "Black Marsha," a theatrical drag queen who often wore garlands of flowers in her hair. She later changed her stage name to Marsha P. Johnson, and said the P. stood for "pay it no mind." Johnson was present at the Stonewall Uprising and played a major role in the gay rights movement. She earned her living through sex work and by performing onstage with drag troupes such as Angels of Light and Hot Peaches. Johnson was a founding member of the Gay Liberation Front and cofounded the Street Transvestite Action Revolutionaries (S.T.A.R.) with her close friend Sylvia Riviera. They later opened STAR House, a shelter for homeless LGBTQ+ teens in Greenwich Village. She was also an AIDS activist with ACT UP from 1987–1992. Known as "the mayor of Christopher Street" due to her welcoming presence in Greenwich Village, Johnson was a popular part of New York City's art scene and modeled for Andy Warhol. She was found dead in the Hudson River in 1992. Police initially ruled the case a suicide, but further investigation led the to reclassify the cause of her death as "undetermined."

CIARA:
"Education Is Your Power"

Ciara is an American singer, songwriter, dancer, and model. She was born in 1985 in Fort Hood, Texas. She traveled the world during her childhood in a military family, but eventually moved to Atlanta, Georgia, where she joined the girl group Hearsay. Her debut album, *Goodies*, earned four Grammy Award nominations and was certified triple platinum. Since her musical debut in 2004, Ciara has had eight *Billboard Hot 100* top ten singles. She has won three BET Awards, three MTV Video Music Awards, and one Grammy Award. She says, "Education is everything—education is your power, education is your way in life for whatever you want to do." Ciara has always kept her personal life private but in recent years has been sharing her beautiful love story with the world, one that encourages women to never settle in love!

VANESSA WILLIAMS:
There She Is

Vanessa Williams, representing the state of New York, became the first Black woman crowned as Miss America. When nude photos were leaked to the press and Williams stepped down, runner-up Suzette Charles, who represented New Jersey and was also a Black American, assumed the title. Three additional Black Americans have been crowned Miss America: Debbye Turner in 1990, Marjorie Vincent in 1991, and Kimberly Aiken in 1994.

ADUT AKECH:
Beautiful Inside and Out

Modeling superstar **Adut Akech** was born in South Sudan; when she was six, she, along with her mother and siblings, emigrated to Australia as refugees. She was scouted multiple times at a young age but did not become a model until she was sixteen years old. She has been on the cover of *Vogue* several times, including the coveted September issue. In 2019, Akech was named "Model of the Year" at the British Fashion Awards.

———

Mixed-race supermodel **Adwoa** (whose name means "born on Monday") signed with Storm Model Management when she was just sixteen years old. She has appeared on the covers of many notable fashion magazines including the British, American, Polish, and Italian editions of *Vogue* magazine. Having been introduced to fashion at an early age, Adwoa has used her platform to be frank about her battles with bipolar disorder, addiction, depression, and her attempted suicide. Her constant highs and lows inspired her in 2015 to launch a female-focused web hub called Gurls Talk. Its mission is to serve as a platform where young girls can openly share their experiences with mental health, body image, and sexuality in a comfortable, trusting, and safe environment. Besides modeling and Gurls Talk, in Adwoa's spare time, she travels to schools across the globe to speak to young girls about depression and other issues.

TYRA BANK/:
America's Top Model

Tyra Banks is a model, businesswoman, producer, writer, and the first Black woman to be featured on the covers of *GQ* and the *Sports Illustrated Swimsuit Issue*. Born in 1973 in Inglewood, California, Banks had a difficult time growing up and was even teased for her ugly duckling looks, telling *HuffPost Live*, "When I was eleven years old, I grew three inches and lost thirty pounds in three months.... [I was] weighing ninety-eight pounds and just looking sick and frail." She was later rejected by four different modeling agencies before she found work, but once she began posing for photos for some of the world's premiere fashion designers and photographers, her career took off. Models. com ranks her as one of only seventeen supermodels. Banks used her modeling career to cross over into different fields, including acting, reality television, her own talk show, and writing. She appeared in the films *Coyote Ugly* and *Halloween: Resurrection*, among others. A successful talk show host, her self-named program ran for five years and won two Emmy Awards. She also created the popular reality series *America's Next Top Model*, as well as serving as executive producer, chief judge, and host of the show for twenty-two seasons. Besides her work in modeling, film, and television, Banks is a bestselling author as well; her young adult novel *Modelland* topped the *New York Times* bestseller list in 2011. She has hosted the popular reality contest show *Dancing with the Stars* since 2020, the first Black woman to have done so, as well as contributing to running the show as an executive producer. The iconic Tyra Banks is consistently ranked as one of the top 100 influential people in the world by *TIME* magazine.

IMAN ABDULMAJID:
All Shades

Iman Abdulmajid, known professionally as **Iman**, is a Somali-born fashion model, actress, and entrepreneur. She was born in 1955 in Mogadishu, Somalia; at the age of four, her parents sent her to attend boarding school in Egypt. Her mother was a gynecologist, while her father was a diplomat and the ambassador to Saudi Arabia. While still at university in Egypt, Iman was discovered by photographer Peter Bears and relocated to the United States to pursue modeling. She graced the cover of *Vogue* in 1976—her very first modeling engagement!—and quickly became a sought-after supermodel. She came to be considered the muse of a number of designers, including Donna Karan, Issey Miyake, Halston, Gianni Versace, and Calvin Klein, and Yves St. Laurent once described her as his "dream woman." After nearly two decades in modeling, in 1994, Iman launched her own cosmetics line, focusing on shades that were difficult to find; in 2010, her business made $25 million. She also successfully launched a line of clothing on the Home Shopping Network (HSN), which has been an ongoing success with an initial focus on embroidered caftans inspired by her childhood in Somalia and Egypt. Iman has also had a successful acting career. She appeared in *Star Trek VI: The Undiscovered Country* as a shapeshifting alien and has also played roles in TV shows such as *Miami Vice* and *In the Heat of the Night*. Iman was married to musician David Bowie from 1992 until his death in 2016.

YARA SHAHIDI:
Actress Activist

Yara Shahidi is an American actress, producer, model, and social activist. She was born in 2000 in Minneapolis, Minnesota. Her father is Iranian, and her mother is mixed Black and Choctaw Indian. When she was four years old, her family moved to California for her father's career as a photographer, which included long-term work for the performer Prince. Shahidi began her acting career when she was just six years old, starring in commercials for such clients as Ralph Lauren, Target, Guess Kids, McDonald's, Disney, and The Children's Place. Her first film role was in *Imagine That* with Eddie Murphy in 2009; the next year, she

appeared in *Salt* with Angelina Jolie. In 2012, Shahidi joined the cast of the TV series *The First Family*, playing Chloe Johnson, the president's daughter. She became well known in 2014 for portraying fourteen-year-old Zoey Johnson on the award-winning sitcom *Black-ish*, a role that earned her a NAACP Image Award in 2014. In 2017, Shahidi was cast as the lead in a *Black-ish* spinoff called *Grown-ish*; the next year, she began studies at Harvard University. One of her recommendation letters was written by former First Lady Michelle Obama. That same year, she also founded Eighteen x 18 with social news publisher NowThis to encourage voting in the midterm elections. She expanded her activism to efforts to increase representation of marginalized groups by forming a production company with her mother in 2020 in connection with ABC Studios. The aim of the company, called 7th Sun, is to produce and distribute content across cable and other broadcast platforms such as streaming services. Shahidi also founded Yara's Club with the Young Women's Leadership Network to provide online mentoring to impoverished children in the hopes of ending poverty through education. She has said, "I think the reason that I try and remain hopeful is I'm watching my peers innovate and find new ways of doing things that are even more efficient than they were before."

Transforming Perceptions

It has long been taboo in the Black community to be openly queer. LGBTQ+ folks are more likely to suffer from homophobic attacks if they are Black. These folks are changing the perception of what it means to openly be themselves in a world that doesn't always respect them.

Gloria Allen ("Mama Gloria") was a transgender rights activist. Born in 1945, she knew that she was female from an early age and even found support from some family members. Although she experienced violence in her youth in high school, she went on to open a charm school for LGBTQ+ youth in Chicago circa 2012. The school has since closed, but besides teaching young people lessons in etiquette, it helped young people find a place where they were accepted. She had gender affirming surgery when she was thirty-seven years old. Mama Gloria spoke publicly about the risks for transgender people of falling victim to violence and advocated for their civil rights. She was part of the Chicago ballroom scene, which grew during the Harlem Renaissance as Black churches banished LGBTQ+ members from their congregations. Rather than going quietly, queer people in that community fostered a sense of belonging by staging elaborate costume balls where they could dress as they liked (often in stunning ball gowns and other elaborate ensembles). The members of these groups formed "families" of sorts—chosen families with "mothers" and "fathers" who looked out for their "children." It is reported that she passed away while sleeping peacefully in her Chicago residence at the LGBTQ+ welcoming Town Hall Apartments in the summer of 2022. Mama Gloria is the subject of a 2020 documentary named for her by Black filmmaker Luchina Fisher.

Tracey Africa is the first Black trans model to achieve prominence. She was born in 1952 and grew up in Newark, New Jersey. She was discovered after sneaking into a fashion shoot with photographer Irvin Penn; he went on to photograph her for the Italian edition of *Vogue*. Soon after, she landed a contract modeling for Clairol Hair Color and appeared on their product packaging. She also modeled for Avon and was the face of one of their skin care lines. In 1980, while on a photo shoot for *Essence* magazine, Africa was outed for being a trans woman; the editor refused to publish photos of her because trans models were at the time considered taboo for a magazine aimed at a female readership. Africa moved to Paris, where she signed a six-month contract with Balenciaga, but then found it difficult to find work after the *Essence* debacle. She returned to New York and signed with a talent agency, but again, there was no work for her since she had been outed. She took up performing in a trans burlesque review. In December 2015, *New York* magazine published an article about Africa's life, which revitalized her career. She was contacted by Clairol, who announced they had chosen her to be the face of their Nice 'N' Easy "Color As Real As You Are" campaign. In 2016, Tracey Africa and Geena Rocero became the first two openly trans models to appear on the cover of *Harper's Bazaar*.

Leyna Bloom is a trans model of Filipina and Black heritage. She was the first trans woman of color to appear in *Vogue India* and on the cover of *Sports Illustrated*'s swimsuit issue. Bloom was born in Chicago, Illinois, to a Black father and Filipina mother. Her mother was deported when she was young, so her father raised her by himself. Growing up, the family was poor and struggled with housing insecurity. Bloom won a scholarship to the Chicago Academy of the Arts and was planning to train as a dancer, but the institution refused to recognize her as a woman, so she moved to New York to take up modeling. Besides modeling, Bloom is an actress who has appeared in the film *Port Authority* and on the final season of FX's *Pose* as Pretentia Khan. Bloom is an activist who supports Black Lives Matter by attending protests and fighting for equality.

Indya Moore is a transgender, nonbinary actor and model. They are best known for playing the role of Angel Evangelista in the FX series *Pose*. Moore, who was born in 1997 in the Bronx, was assigned the male gender at birth but identifies as female. They are of Haitian, Dominican, and Puerto Rican ancestry. Their parents were transphobic, and they left home at the age of fourteen and entered foster care. They dropped out of high school because of bullying and eventually earned a high school equivalency degree. They began modeling at the age of fifteen for such high-profile clients as Gucci and Dior, despite the risk of hiring a trans model for fashion shoots. But as their career went on, Moore became disenchanted with the modeling business because of its emphasis on a specific body type. They were encouraged to go into acting and auditioned for the independent film *Saturday Church*. Moore landed the role of Dijon in the film, which was screened at the Tribeca Film Festival, receiving broader distribution in 2018. This led to more modeling contracts and more acting roles, including the role of Angel, a transgender sex worker, on *Pose*. Moore has appeared on the cover of *Vogue* twice in one year, 2020 (India and Spain). They are an outspoken advocate for marginalized communities and are politically active.

Black dancers and models have challenged the norm when it comes to the aesthetics of beauty. Dancers have had to fight their way to the top of their profession through sheer willpower. In a world that doesn't even have shoes that come in your color, challenging the stereotypical norm of the anemic, underfed dancer is quite a feat. The same can be said of those Black women who broke into modeling at a time when Twiggy was gracing the covers of the glossy fashion supplements with her blue eyes, blonde hair, and rail-thin physique. These pioneers graced the cover of *Vogue* despite looking different than other models of the time, facing down prejudice, and along the way taught us to appreciate their beauty and grace.

BUT WAIT, THERE'S SO MUCH MORE

We hope you've enjoyed learning about all the awesome Black women we've featured. Researching their biographies for this project was a real joy and definitely an eye-opener. We've racked our brains trying to find the most relevant categories to give you a good overview of how Black women have been and still are reshaping the world, but we know there's so much more than what we could cover in a single volume. It is important to remember as well that there's a historical gap lasting approximately 400 years when many Black women were not recorded as actively making history because they were enslaved. The accomplishments and potential of these women are lost to this blank spot in history.

The history of Black women in America is still largely being written. New discoveries about our shared past are still happening today. Who knows what artifacts are still lying undisturbed in someone's attic? There's a good chance that another novel like *Our Nig* (1859) by **Harriet Wilson** is waiting to be found and cherished for the insight it gives us into our collective past.

We have come a long way since the days of slavery, but we still have a long way to go toward ensuring that every Black woman has the opportunity to meet her potential. Hopefully, reading about the women in this book has given you a new appreciation for awesome Black women and a few of their accomplishments.

Because there are so many awesome Black women, unfortunately, it wasn't possible for us to include all of their accomplishments in this one book. But we would love to hear your nominations of other awesome Black women who could be featured and praised in future books. We look forward to hearing your nominations: Who are your awesome Black women?

To Learn More:

The National Archives for Black Women's History is the largest repository solely dedicated to the collection and preservation of material relating to African American women. The collection includes correspondence, photographs, and speeches. For further information, please call the Mary McLeod Bethune Council House National Historic Site at 301-832-3977, or for more information, see its page on the National Park Service web site: https://www.nps.gov/mamc/learn/historyculture/mamc_nabwh.htm

WHO ARE YOUR AWESOME WOMEN?

Dear Reader,

This book almost never made it to the printer because we kept finding more and more fascinating females deserving to be honored in the annals of history. We would love to have a follow-up volume detailing the lives and times of more role models. We invite you to email, tweet, or send a note with your nomination of your Awesome Women. We would love to hear from you about this and continue the celebration of these "great unknowns" who didn't make it into the history books UNTIL NOW!

Below is a simple nomination form, and we would love to credit you, so please include your contact information. Thanks for your participation - you are pretty awesome, yourself!

xoxo

Becca and M.J.

- -

I Nominate the Following Awesome Woman:

_____

_____

_____

_____

_____

Mango Publishing 2850 Douglas Road
4th Floor, Coral Gables, Florida 33134

Twitter: @MangoPublishing
Email: support@mangopublishinggroup.com

ABOUT THE AUTHORS

Becca Anderson comes from a long line of preachers and teachers from Ohio and Kentucky. The teacher side of her family led her to become a women's studies scholar and the author of *The Book of Awesome Women*. An avid collector of meditations, prayers, and blessings, she helps run a "Gratitude and Grace" virtual circle that meets weekly. In non-pandemic times, she gives gratitude workshops at churches and bookstores in the San Francisco Bay Area, where she currently resides. Becca Anderson credits her spiritual practice with helping her recover from cancer and wants to share this healing wisdom with anyone who is facing difficulty in their life.

Born in Port-au-Prince, **M.J. Fievre**, BS Ed, is a long-time educator and writer. M.J. earned a bachelor's degree in education from Barry University. A seasoned K–12 teacher, she spent much time building up her students, helping them feel comfortable in their own skin, and affirming their identities. She has taught creative writing workshops to children at the O, Miami Poetry Festival and the Miami Art

Museum, as well as in various schools in Santa Cruz de la Sierra (Bolivia), Port-au-Prince (Haiti), and South Florida. As the ReadCaribbean program coordinator for the prestigious Miami Book Fair, M.J. also directs and produces the children's cultural show *Taptap Krik? Krak!*

Mango Publishing, established in 2014, publishes an eclectic list of books by diverse authors—both new and established voices—on topics ranging from business, personal growth, women's empowerment, LGBTQ+ studies, health, and spirituality to history, popular culture, time management, decluttering, lifestyle, mental wellness, aging, and sustainable living. We were recently named 2019 *and* 2020's #1 fastest-growing independent publisher by *Publishers Weekly*. Our success is driven by our main goal, which is to publish high-quality books that will entertain readers as well as make a positive difference in their lives.

Our readers are our most important resource; we value your input, suggestions, and ideas. We'd love to hear from you—after all, we are publishing books for you!

Please stay in touch with us and follow us at:

Facebook: Mango Publishing
Twitter: @MangoPublishing
Instagram: @MangoPublishing
LinkedIn: Mango Publishing
Pinterest: Mango Publishing
Newsletter: mangopublishinggroup.com/newsletter

Join us on Mango's journey to reinvent publishing, one book at a time.

Printed in the USA
CPSIA information can be obtained
at www.ICGtesting.com
JSHW032339241123
52664JS00025B/128